Where's Home?

In Nova Scotia, the answer can be complicated.

Jan Fancy Hull

Cover painting: "The Big Hill on #7 Highway" by Christine Heggelin

Back cover:

> Above, "Between Two Places", hooked rug by Deanne Fitzpatrick

> Below, "Safe As Houses", quilt art by Valerie Hearder

Author photo on page 157 by Betty Meredith

Editor: Andrew Wetmore

ISBN: 978-1-9992687-2-5

First edition June, 2020

MOOSE HOUSE
PUBLICATIONS

397 Parker Mountain Road
Granville Ferry NS
B0S 1A0

moosehousepress.com
info@moosehousepress.com

We live and work in Mi'kma'ki, the ancestral and unceded territory of the Mi'kmaq People. This territory is covered by the "Treaties of Peace and Friendship" which Mi'kmaq and Wolastoqiyik (Maliseet) People first signed with the British Crown in 1725. The treaties did not deal with surrender of lands and resources but in fact recognized Mi'kmaq and Wolastoqiyik (Maliseet) title and established the rules for what was to be an ongoing relationship between nations. We are all Treaty people.

Foreword

This book is the result of conversations with Nova Scotians over several years. It draws on surveys, one-on-one interviews, and the work of selected writers and artists.

Brief descriptions of several individuals and topics, with links to online sources for further reading, are at my website, **janfancyhull.ca**.

Two kinds of contributions appear in boxes in the text:

Survey response

Anonymous responses to the online survey
described in the appendix
appear in a box, in italics.

Other material, ranging from the lyrics of a song to an extract from a blog, appears in plain text:

The title
by this author, in this publication

The text, which may run on for a page or more.

The Appendix describes my research process.

Preface

This is a Nova Scotia-centric book. Unless I state that they're in some other part of the world, all the places I name in this book are in Nova Scotia.

I may have assumed that you are more familiar with Nova Scotia than you are. Readers from away may want to become more familiar with this Canadian Province.

The simplest research may expand but not clarify your vision of this place. Here's what you would find on Wikipedia:

> Nova Scotia is one of Canada's three Maritime Provinces, and one of the four provinces that form Atlantic Canada. Its provincial capital is Halifax. Nova Scotia is the second-smallest of Canada's ten provinces, with an area of 55,284 square kilometres (21,300 sq mi), including Cape Breton and another 3,800 coastal islands. As of 2016, the population was 923,598. Nova Scotia is Canada's second-most-densely populated province, after Prince Edward Island, with 17.4 inhabitants per square kilometre (45/sq mi).

That's as useful as introducing myself by telling you who my parents and siblings and neighbours are, and what's my blood type. It tells very little about who we are.

In Nova Scotia, though, introducing yourself by naming your connections to family and place is not so unusual. We like to be located, so you might hear a Nova Scotian introduce herself as "Rae and Marjorie's daughter" before she gives her own name.

We like to locate strangers, too, either by community or family of origin, so they're not strangers any longer, they're just two or three degrees separated from someone or somewhere we know or knew.

I was stopped at a traffic light in Florida when a vehicle in the next lane drew up. The driver rolled down his window and shouted, "Where?" evidently having seen my licence plate. We called our hometowns and favourite hangouts back and forth until the non-Nova Scotians behind us blew their horns for us to get a move on.

Nova Scotians are rarely as far apart as the theoretical six degrees of separation, if you pay attention to the clues. Facebook could have been invented for Nova Scotians, as it does a good job of showing us the friends of our friends, some of whom we will recognize as our friends. It's a handy reference.

What, then, are we to make of those whose answer to "Where's home for you?" is some faraway place where we can't place the family name, and the accent is unfamiliar? Even in little Nova Scotia, that faraway place might be in the next county, or those new people who moved in next door, with whom we may not share a mother tongue or customs. The 2011 Census says that Nova Scotians claim over thirty different mother tongues, including sign language.

Do we say let's just be welcoming and make new friends anyway? Some do. Some do not.

We like to fit in. Even when our ancestors lived in caves, I'm sure they preferred to be welcomed as they approached the mouth of that cave rather than be driven off with threatening gestures.

Some of us like to stick out, too. We want to excel, to lead, to learn, to do new things in new ways. We may have to leave the familiarities of home and the confines of our province to find those opportunities which make us feel like life is worth living. Are we sad to go? Some are.

Or some don't go, and are sad, remaining 'hungry inside for the wide world outside,' as Ron Hynes wrote in his ballad 'Sonny's Dream'.

Newcomers experiencing Nova Scotia's kinds of hospitality must be forgiven for wondering just what is going on. Are we friendly? Yes, we certainly are, and if you don't agree we'll fight you. Are we welcoming? Sure, you're welcome to come here, and help out, or stay out of the way.

I don't conclude the book in the way that you might expect, with a sweet summary that draws us all together and wraps us in the Nova Scotia flag. I can't do that because we don't live our lives in averages and aggregations. We are individuals. We do have habits and perspectives in common with others, of course; but you can't know a person until you meet the person, any more than you know a grandmother or a snowplow driver by what bread they like to eat, or don't.

That's what this book will show you. There are nearly one million people living in this province, and we're like snowflakes – no two exactly alike. There would be more of us, but so many have gone away, and for many different reasons. Read on, and you will hear from many 'ordinary' Nova Scotians. If you agree with or like some and not others, that is natural. In fact, if you arrive here from elsewhere, and proclaim that you just love every Nova Scotian 'cause we're so down-to-earth that you'd like to pinch our cheeks, we'll know in our hearts that you are loving some caricature of us, but not us, not me.

Because we ourselves don't love all of us. If it were possible, we'd be doing it.

When you meet the next new-to-you person in Nova Scotia, perhaps you'll have a broader understanding of what I believe is the message everyone in this book is sending: to simultaneously hold them close and give them room.

Perhaps they'll do the same for you.

Introduction: Voices

"I felt like the land knew me," says a woman who lives on land her family has owned for two centuries. "There's a genuine openness here," says a ten-year resident.

"I'm surprised that people seem surprised to meet their neighbours."

"I told my kids, 'If you can't find something good about everyone in this community, there's something wrong with you.'"

"The people who live on this street don't want you here."

"My first spring was grey, depressing, utterly unlike anything I'd experienced."

"The locals warmed up once they saw we were staying."

"You can make a decision to like it anywhere."

"You can't feel welcomed in a community unless you get involved."

"I have roots elsewhere but I am rooted here."

What does home mean for Nova Scotians, both residents in the province and those who have "gone down the road"? What thrills us about this province, and what disappoints? Are we a friendly bunch or stand-offish? Must we have generations in a graveyard nearby to feel we belong? Does a magnificent landscape make up for wretched weather two seasons of the year?

In this book you'll hear the voices of Nova Scotians old and new, whose connections to home are as varied as our landscape. Our histories, struggles, and interests are dissimilar, but most of us agree that Nova Scotia's a special place to call home. Maybe we agree about that because of our differences.

Why did I set out to write about Nova Scotia as "home"? I was born and raised and earned a good living here, but took the province mostly for granted until I began spending the cold half of each year in Florida – yes, a cliché, and a nice one, too. While exiled in the land of sun'n'fun, I found myself haunting webcams for views of home, watching skaters on the Oval in Halifax, behaving more like a crow on a cold wire than a snowbird on a warm beach. I was homesick for winter, for places and people I care about, and for my lakeside log home.

Now I'm back home year-round and my calendar contains the seasons I missed: the late fall, winter's snow and deep cold, and spring's "rain, drizzle, fog, ice, sleet" that you'll read about in these pages. As with people, there are good and bad attributes in any place. Some of us may need time to sort out which of them matter most so we can trust our compass when it points to home. I learned that home is more than just a happy place.

Where's home? The question is simple; the answers can be complicated. Enjoy the conversations.

-Jan Fancy Hull

Here's where
this book
takes you

North
Sydney

Glace Bay

Baddeck

Whycocomagh

Antigonish

Boat
Harbour

Pictou

Canso

Truro

Amherst

New
Germany

West
Chezzetcook

Barss
Corner

Cherry Brook

Upper New
Cornwall
Bridgetown

Halifax

Mahone Bay

Kejimkujik
National
Park

Bridgewater

Lunenburg

Kingsburg

Freeport

Broad
Cove

Petit
Ruisseau

Vogler's Cove

Yarmouth

Birchtown

This is all part of *Mi'kma'ki*, the
traditional land of the Mi'qmaq
and Maliseet peoples

Table of contents

Jan Fancy Hull

1 – Our Nova Scotia Home

Survey responses

Life is good here. I wouldn't want to live anywhere else.
<>
Love the friendly people and down home atmosphere.

History and heritage

Jay LeBlanc feels a deep attachment to her home. She grew up in Ontario; but when Jay was fifteen, her family moved to her father's ancestral Acadian village of Petit-Ruisseau in the District of Clare. Once there, she knew she had found where she belonged.

"I say I'm from here," she tells me, gesturing around her house and at the property outside her window. "This is the land of my ancestors, my relatives on my father's side. The house is almost two hundred years old. I feel like the land here is my land."

Petit-Ruisseau retained its Acadian culture and language. "I felt I belonged," Jay says. "I felt an outsider, too, being English-speaking in a French community, but I felt like the land knew me."

The Municipality of the District of Clare, the western half of Digby County, is the only municipality in Nova Scotia today that conducts business and offers services in both English and French. Jay prefers to say her address is Petit-Ruisseau on Baic Sainte-Marie, not Little Brook in Clare, which is named for a county in Ireland.

Vanessa Fells was born in Yarmouth (pop. 6,500), and her family house there felt like home – when she was inside it. "But outside the house you could feel you weren't wanted, didn't belong."

Vanessa and her family are African Nova Scotians. "My sister and I and our family lived in the middle of town. One time we were

15

playing on the street outside our own house. The cops drove up, stopped, and told us, 'The people who live on this street don't want you here.'"

The Fells girls, back in the day.

What's the effect of growing up with racist comments like that?

"If you don't feel at home in your own community," she says, "you're on defence all the time."

Vanessa had homeschooling to start her education. "I never even realized there were people not like me until I went to public school, and then I wondered, 'What's happening?'"

Coming from a long line of educators, her family emphasized the importance of a good education. She took this to heart, completing two Bachelor's degrees in six years, and in 2013 she completed a Masters of Education at Mount Saint Vincent University in Halifax.

Now, as an adult, she identifies with a stronger community. "My home is the Black community," she says. "I'm proud of my ancestors and what they did for me."

Survey response

When people move here and cut off access to beaches and trails that have been open and accessible for hundreds of years, they have started off on the wrong foot. It is not accepted nor liked by the local people. They are resented. It is not the way here.

That's not nice. It happens, though. With settlements dating from before the sixteen hundreds and Indigenous people here for thousands of years before that, there are many old and unofficial paths, trails, and roads which have served for generations. Over the years, land has been surveyed and sold to buyers who assume they have every right to fence in their property and, intentionally or not, to fence out the locals.

Some Nova Scotian property deeds go back as far as land grants from King George III, and subsequent divisions and bequests were not always accurately recorded. Defending title to your land can be a frightening, frustrating, expensive process: someone makes a claim against it to clear the title and you must prove they don't own it and you do. Having a deed in your hand helps immensely, though not entirely, especially if it describes property 'beginning at a stake on the south-west bank of the stream and thence...' The old wooden stake has long ago rotted away, the trees that were blazed have grown tall or fallen, and the stream may dry up in the summers.

If you are descended from the colonial settlers, you may be surprised to learn that there are remnants of ancient wars still to be reconciled in Nova Scotia. If you are of African or Indigenous descent, you likely know this all too well.

Following the American War of Independence, 1776-1783, and the War of 1812, some 30,000 Loyalists came to Nova Scotia from the United States. They were granted land as a reward for their loyalty to the British Crown. Yet some descendants of the 3,000 Black Loyalists included in that wave of loyal refugees have lived on their land without clear title ever since. Taxes were assessed, of course, and were paid, no doubt. But without clear title, you can't sell your land, nor use it as collateral for a loan or mortgage, or pass it down to the next generation in confidence.

Clarifying land titles is an expensive legal process. In 2017, the Nova Scotia Land Titles Initiative began to help residents in the communities of North Preston, East Preston, Lake Loon/Cherry Brook, Lincolnville, and Sunnyville receive clear title to their land, and the government has pledged to cover all costs. In June 2019 the CBC reported that 144 applications had been received, representing 180 parcels of land of an estimated thousands of parcels. Legal aid lawyers and surveyors have begun this challenging work.

Meanwhile, the question must be asked: whose land was it that was granted to all those Loyalists? There had been non-indigenous fishers, traders, and settlers in the land of Mi'kmaki for a couple of centuries. The French and English fought bitterly for control of the region, and the Indigenous peoples were beneficiaries, pawns, or victims in the battles.

Several Peace and Friendship Treaties were signed between 1725 and 1779, mostly to do with trade and the right of the Indigenous people to earn a modest living. Their rights to land and resources were not ceded.

In the 21st century, some institutions begin their gatherings by acknowledging whose land they do business on and benefit from. Canadian universities have published their recommended statements after consultation with various aboriginal academic staff. Most statements are similar to this:

> We [I] would like to begin by acknowledging that we are in Mi'kma'ki, the ancestral and unceded territory of the

Mi'kmaq People. This territory is covered by the Treaties of Peace and Friendship which Mi'kmaq and Wolastoqiyik (Maliseet) People first signed with the British Crown in 1725. The treaties did not deal with surrender of lands and resources but in fact recognized Mi'kmaq and Wolastoqiyik (Maliseet) title and established the rules for what was to be an ongoing relationship between nations.

Dalhousie University in Halifax adds this: 'We are all Treaty people.'

There can be no such thing as a brief history of Nova Scotia that is also accurate, and I am not attempting to present one here. Any historical references are here to illustrate that it's complex. I do believe I was taught a 'brief history' in school, the kind that leaves out all the bits that are uncomfortable and uncomplimentary for whoever is telling it.

Our history can be confusing, as Nova Scotia was once considered a choice prize to be won, retained or regained by multiple military forces. But as you read even some of the details, especially those with roots that are many centuries long, you may gain some understanding of 'why those people are the way they are.'

Lands are invaded, people are oppressed, time and time again. This seems to be the history of all nations. But no nation achieves its potential while the rights and homelands of any of its people are neglected.

Survey response

> *My family moved from one very small community to a
> community near Halifax when I was 15.*
> *My old community was mainly Protestant whereas the new one
> was mainly RC [Roman Catholic]. One or two neighbours visited
> my mother to advise that her girls were not welcome to become
> friendly with their sons.*

Many, but not all, Catholic communities in Nova Scotia are also French/Acadian. One is West Chezzetcook, on "the western end of the Eastern Shore," as Beverly Hugli likes to describe it.

I met Beverly there in early December when the marsh grasses were a study in brown under a pewter sky. The land is low, tidal waters come to the roadside, and the tallest feature, visible from most of the village, is the spire on Saint Anselm's Catholic Church. Though West Chezzetcook is an historic Acadian settlement, the church is not called Église Saint-Anselm, because the residents don't speak French.

They once did, of course, Beverly explains. But in the middle of the last century, "Officially, it was stressed that we had to forget 'that French' or we'd never make it in life," she says. "French schools were cut out in Nova Scotia. French was taught as a foreign language, just another subject. The parish priests and the nuns who taught us in school did what they could to preserve our language and culture. One amazing nun, Sister Claude Colombière from Wedgeport, taught French to thirty-five kids every day after school."

Beverly invited me to meet her in La Grange, one of the buildings at L'Acadie de Chezzetcook, *site historique acadien*. "This Musée is a heritage property," she says with pride. "People here 'of a certain age' got together to create it. A lot of residents here are Mi'kmaq and Métis, too. In recent years, they started to research their history, and people are discovering their heritage."

In West Chezzetcook, if you were French you were most likely Roman Catholic. "Religion had a lot to do with it," Beverly says. "You didn't marry outside your religion in the old days. After the war [WWII], men had cars, so they were able to leave the village, and some married English women." Some of those English women would have been Protestant, thus pillars of language and religious heritage began to erode, peacefully, for love.

On the other hand, after Beverly moved to Dartmouth in the sixties to teach school, "I bought a car, so I could come back home to West Chezzetcook and commute." She taught for twenty-nine years, and in the evenings she taught French to adults, just as Sister Claude had done for the West Chezzetcook children in the mid-fifties.

When people 'of a certain age' are the active group in a community, does it mean the community will decline when they're gone? "There are a lot of elderly widows here," Beverly says, "and as they die, their houses are bought by people such as the surfers attracted to nearby Lawrencetown Beach. So we have carpenters, painters – young people – moving in. Their children go to school, but schools are not in the village now, and the new people are not necessarily church-goers. Older people are the volunteers now."

Does Beverly Hugli think life was better in the old days?

"I'm not sure," she replies. "We are the generation that saw major changes – electricity, cars – everything changed so fast. Trains used to come from Halifax all the way to Musquodoboit Harbour, so we had public transit. You didn't need a lot of money to travel on the train, to take your clams and other produce to the market in Halifax." You did need a lot of money to buy cars, though, so those who wanted cars needed to move to where there were jobs that paid more than clam-digging did.

As Beverly and I conclude our interview in La Grange at the Musée, a dozen or so West Chezzetcook women join us. They're here for the weekly gathering of *La Club Français de Chezzetcook*, which Beverly leads. Many are those 'of a certain age' who were attending school when French was legislated away. They've come to learn everyday phrases in their mother tongue so they can converse with relatives, especially grandchildren, in French-speaking communities in Nova Scotia, New Brunswick and Quebec.

The gentle woman seated next to me tells me softly that she was in Grade Two "when it happened." Her schooling had been in French, but one day they were ordered to speak only English, a foreign language. I'm reminded of Vanessa Fells' account of her first day in public school in Yarmouth, in a class with white classmates for the first time, wondering, "What's happening?"

"So, why learn French now, at your age and stage?" I ask La Club Français members.

"It's our heritage," says one. "I have regrets that English was pushed to the exclusion of our own language," says another.

Others mention their desire to communicate with relatives who do speak French, perhaps exclusively, in their homes. Someone says she is gaining a sense of pride in her heritage through her ability to speak French. Nobody speaks with acrimony, just determination and a sense of achievement. La langue française won't die out on their watch. Most aren't fluent, and may never be, but learning some common phrases will make telephone conversations possible and bring their loved ones closer.

La Club members are preparing for a Christmas concert. Beverly has brought a player and a CD of French Christmas carols which they'll sing for the community's children, who are the age they were when "that French" was prohibited in school. "And then we'll give them cookies!" Some traditions are universal.

The carol they're rehearsing as I leave has a familiar tune – Jingle Bells – but the story is much different from the English version about the sleigh that gets upsot.

Vive le vent (tune: Jingle Bells)

French	*English* (literal translation
(Refrain)	

Vive le vent, vive le vent,	Long live the wind, long live the
Vive le vent d'hiver,	wind,
Qui s'en va sifflant, soufflant	Long live the winter wind,
Dans les grands sapins verts,	Which goes whistling, blowing
oh !	In the big green Christmas trees,
	oh!
Vive le temps, vive le temps,	Long live the weather, long live
Vive le temps d'hiver,	the weather,
Boules de neige et Jour de l'An	Long live the winter weather,
Et Bonne Année grand-mère !	Snowballs and New Year's Day
	and Happy New Year, Grandma!
Sur le long chemin	Along the long path
Tout blanc de neige blanche	All white from the white snow
Un vieux monsieur s'avance	An old man advances
Avec sa canne dans la main.	With his cane in his hand.
Et tout là-haut le vent	And all above the wind
Qui siffle dans les branches	Which whistles in the branches
Lui souffle la romance	Blows on him the romance
Qu'il chantait petit enfant,	That he sang as a young child,
oh !	oh!

Refrain

My pleasant visit to West Chezzetcook was in December 2017. On Remembrance Day in 2018, parishioners learned suddenly that their beloved Saint Anselm's church was closed to them. This notice still appears on the Archdiocese website:

PLEASE NOTE: The Saint Anselm church building has been temporarily closed due to extensive mould in the building causing a major health issue. The regularly scheduled 11:00 AM Mass at Saint Anselm will be moved to Saint Anne in Lake Echo. For more options click one of the Associated Parishes below.

Many churches in Nova Scotia have had to close. Dwindling congregations find it impossible to support the cost of maintaining what is often the largest structure in their community, built in a different time. However, Saint Anselm's boasts 400 parishioners, not dwindling by any measure of which I'm aware.

Parishioners formed a registered society, Friends of Saint Anselm's, to appeal to the Archdiocese to permit them back in the sanctuary. They demonstrated at Saint Mary's Basilica in Halifax, formed a 'living chain' around their church on the one-year anniversary of the closure, and have been fundraising to support costs of their appeal. I didn't find any official response.

Being locked out of their church without warning or comment must be deeply discouraging, and may have felt to some like it was an echo of that day, when they were little children, being locked out of their mother tongue.

For Beverly Hugli and parishioners in West Chezzetcook, where's home?

Survey response

I love Nova Scotia. I am proud to say I am a Nova Scotian. My father's ancestors came here on the Hector. I think having that long a history in a place has an impact on identity. There is some sort of belonging that is part of who I am.

Now, there's a keen citizen, wrapped in the Nova Scotian flag – an ancient flag featuring a coat of arms granted to the Scottish colony by King Charles 1 in 1625. The ship *Hector* brought settlers to

Pictou from Scotland in 1773, and anyone who can trace their family history to the *Hector* claims deep roots here.

Kathy Rafuse of Middle New Cornwall traces her family history back to the arrival in Nova Scotia of the brigantine *Jane* in 1755. The *Jane* doesn't have the reputation of the *Hector*. In fact, my brief online search didn't find Kathy's ancestor or the *Jane*, but I won't let that stand in the way of a good story.

Here's an excerpt from an account Kathy gave me:

> These three men, Hammond, Lunt, and Hallamore [Kathy's ancestor], were living peacefully in a little seaport town in the south of England...when they were transported to Nova Scotia on the Brig "Jane," about 1755, under command of General Bowyer...not having crew enough he went ashore, picked the three men and forced them to go aboard his ship [impressments or press gang]. There was no choice but to go, and all went well until they landed in Nova Scotia waters. Once there, they waited for a chance to desert.
>
> Now, this is true, coming from the lips of...Hallamore and Hammond. In the dead and darkness of the night they slipped ship and took to the woods. They didn't have far to go before they were among the Indians. Nor was it long before the captain discovered that no Hammond or Hallamore could be found on ship and a searching party was on their trail.
>
> They, however, fell into good hands among the Indians, who, with kindness and skill, hid them by covering them with blankets and sitting on them at times, and soon they dared show themselves in Indian clothes.
>
> Hammond was not his original name...The Indians gave him the name of Hammond because he lived with them on Hammond's Plain...he married a French and Indian girl...
>
> Now, Lunt...went to New Cornwall [Lunenburg County] with Thomas Hallamore, lived and died there, and his bones are lying in the old cemetery in Lower Cornwall under a sour apple tree. He was never married.

> Thomas Cotton Hallamore took his mother's name of Cotton when he became a vagabond or runaway... He had sons and daughters...Hallamore came from a royal family... and in the old days lived in an old and lovely castle in England...lived to be 102.

This story would make a great movie, wouldn't it? It has royal ancestry, fugitives, indigenous people, and press gangs. It includes inter-racial marriage, hospitality to newcomers, leaving it all behind, putting down roots (including final ones under a sour apple tree) and leaving a legacy. Hallamore experienced all that, as countless others did and continue to do, with variations, to the present day.

Today, Hallamore's many-great granddaughter Kathy lives peacefully with her family "on a dirt road off a dirt road," still in Middle New Cornwall, Lunenburg County, in what was "Mum's second cousin Charlie's house," and the communities around are populated with her relatives. Kathy Rafuse doesn't claim any status (or wealth) from being able to trace her heritage to the brig *Jane* or its unwilling 'royal' crew. Instead, she says, "We're all newcomers, some just arrived earlier than others," and she's grateful for how First Nations people welcomed her forebears to Nova Scotia long ago.

Those First Nations people were no match for the superior strength of the invading British forces, who treated them cruelly in their quest to rid this bounteous land of its original population. Murdering them outright eventually fell out of fashion, so church and state forced Indigenous children into deathly so-called residential schools until late into the twentieth century.

When reporting former students' testimony about what was done to them in those schools, many news media today warn us that 'some language may be disturbing.' Indeed, it is.

Meanwhile, in Halifax Harbour, sailors were 'flogged 'round the fleet, a form of punishment in the old days of the British Navy,' according to my copy of *The Oxford Companion to Ships & the Sea:*

For the more serious crimes committed on board...the man undergoing sentence was placed in a boat in which a ship's grating had been lashed upright across the thwarts, and rowed alongside each ship lying in harbour. While bound to the grating, he was given twelve strokes with a cat-o'-nine-tails by a boatswain's mate of the ship off which the boat was lying...

This was carried out at each ship. Not all survived this grisly punishment. No wonder Hallamore and his mates deserted the brig *Jane* at their first opportunity.

In 1755, when the *Jane* was reportedly anchored in Halifax Harbour, the Expulsion of the Acadians, *Le Grand Dérangement*, was transpiring. The British wanted the French Catholic Acadians to swear allegiance to their English Protestant king. Some Acadians offered to pledge neutrality, but this didn't work with other allegiances. This pledge became eroded, and the British decided that the region would be more secure for their purposes if the Acadians were dispersed. Add in the well-armed Mi'kmaq and Maliseet, and there was a lot of forcing, resisting, capturing, fighting back, and murdering as the battles for control of Nova Scotia (which then included what is now New Brunswick) waged on.

Eleven thousand Acadians were deported from their farms. When many of them eventually returned, they found their land had been given away, so they turned to the sea for their living.

Is all this ancient history too heavy and serious for a book about people's struggles to find and keep their homes? All right then, let's take a brief look at the 1917 Halifax Explosion, a tragedy with unintended consequences, featuring a heavily-loaded munitions ship destined for France, and an empty cargo ship, both moving slowly in thick fog in the narrows in Halifax Harbour, where the A. Murray MacKay Bridge is now. They collided, there were sparks, and soon erupted the largest man-made explosion to that moment in the history of the world.

Survey response

*I am here because of the Halifax Explosion, as my grandfather's
first wife was killed that day, so that day has a very special
meaning for me each year.
He re-married and my dad was born, so here I am.*

There was widespread devastation, including 1,600 deaths immediately and more to follow. The good people of Boston were among many who responded to the disaster, sending a train with medical help and supplies. In gratitude for this generosity, Nova Scotia has since 1941 sent a huge Christmas tree to the Boston Common every year.

The Halifax Explosion makes for interesting reading now, a century removed. There are monuments, a bell tower, books, films, and commemorations. Relief funds from far and wide assisted the extensive rebuilding of Halifax and its citizens. Left out when the relief funds were being distributed were a Mi'kmaq settlement, Turtle Grove, on the Dartmouth shore of the harbour, which was obliterated; and the Black village of Africville, on the Halifax side, which received serious damage. If your home is destroyed and left in ruins while others' homes are being rebuilt, you lose ground, perhaps the very ground your home was on.

I will state the obvious: the French and British who figure so large in Nova Scotia's colonial history didn't start here and their original quarrels were not with this land's indigenous inhabitants. The colonists came from another part of the world, where England and France played out merry old hell for centuries, along with or in opposition to many other nations. Much of what happened in Nova Scotia's story has been in response to troubles across the Atlantic Ocean.

Here's one example: an action called the 'eviction of the Gaels', or 'The Clearances' took place between 1750 and 1860 in Scotland. Landlords wanted to combine smallholdings into larger fields suitable for new agricultural practices, so they evicted the clan-member tenants. The tenants had believed they had permanent rights to rent the land, but it had never been written down...this does sound familiar.

So, in 1773, the *Hector*, an old vessel that had seen better days, set out from Scotland with 200 Gaelic-speaking passengers on board. The Scots were encouraged to go aboard the *Hector* with an offer of free passage, their own farms, and a year of provisions in the New World.

The *Hector* measured thirty-three meters in length and under seven meters in width: three school buses long and two buses wide. Accommodations below decks would have been cramped, to say the least. There is an excellent museum and replica of the *Hector* in Pictou. Look into the hold: it boggles the imagination to think of 200 men, women, children, and all their earthly possessions crossing the sea in that small space.

After two harrowing months at sea, including a horrific gale, the *Hector* dropped anchor in Pictou in mid-September with eighteen fewer souls on board, lost to smallpox and dysentery. They had fled from famine, and arrived to forced labour, having to clear land for shelter mere weeks before winter. The free provisions never arrived.

In 1900 there were a recorded 100,000 Gaelic-speakers in Nova Scotia, most born here. By 1930, only 30,000 spoke Gaelic. In 2016, 240 Nova Scotians claimed Scottish Gaelic as their mother tongue.

Even back when whole communities in Nova Scotia spoke Gaelic, mostly in Cape Breton, schools were never permitted to give instruction in that language.

Suppressing a language is an effective way to stifle a culture. Encouraging a language is definitely the road back. Today, anyone can take classes to learn to speak Mi'kmaq, French, Gaelic, languages once censored by our governments. Now, we can enrol children in French immersion schools. We can visit centres dedicated to the histories of our many cultures. Now, we can take pleasure in trying to learn what people were prohibited from doing not so many years ago.

Jan Fancy Hull

Kejimkujik - a view from a canoe

I visited Kejimkujik National Park in 2017; passes were free for everyone that year to commemorate one hundred and fifty years since Canada's Confederation. It's a beautiful park which one hundred and thirty homes were expropriated to create in 1968. Those displaced families may now apply for permanent free passes. No doubt some of those displaced families were Mi'kmaq. One assumes they were paid 'fair market value', but I wonder if they think the park's trilingual signs in French, English, and Mi'kmaq, plus free passes, are adequate compensation for our use and their loss of homeland their ancestors had occupied for thousands of years?

Here's a bright spot: it is no longer federal government policy to expropriate land to create national parks.

I am impressed by the resilience of all the people in our collective history, and their desire to reclaim at least some of what they lost – language, ceremonies, family traditions, dress, religion, dignity, medicine, land, and the right to move freely in their home society. Whenever the people I interviewed touched on these issues, they showed pride in their heritage, and eagerness to revive it.

These stories – and many others – make up the history of Nova Scotia and all Nova Scotians. Events we didn't know about, perhaps omitted or glossed over in our history books, are still part of our collective history. History belongs to all of us, regardless of our language, or skin colour, or religion, whether we are 'born and raised' or came here at three months of age or three months ago, or whether our great-greats were receiving or inflicting the misery.

We can't put Humpty Dumpty back together again, but we can own our shared past and aim to do better from today forward.

Queen Elizabeth II, Christmas Day 2017 (excerpt)

We think of our homes as places of warmth, familiarity, and love – of shared stories and memories – which is perhaps why, at this time of year, so many return to where they grew up. There is a timeless simplicity to the pull of home. For many, the idea of home reaches beyond a physical building, to a home town or city...We expect our homes to be a place of safety – sanctuary, even – which makes it all the more shocking when the comfort they provide is shattered...

Arrivals and departures

Ten percent of those who answered my survey described themselves as 'born and raised' or 'born and bred' Nova Scotians. The word 'born' carries a lot of weight and some powerful rights, including national citizenship, a significant lifetime designation, determined by one arbitrary detail – where the stork delivered you.

Survey responses

I'm from the Valley. My Mum was born in England. She was 6 months old when she came to Canada from England.

<>

When we first moved here I read an obituary about a woman of 101. The first line said, "Born in Boston, moved to Pictou at 3 months..." I looked at my partner and said we're screwed, we will never be considered as anything but outsiders!

Would you have interpreted the obituary that way? To me, it seems to celebrate a small detail in a long story. Just as interesting as being born and bred in Nova Scotia is being born somewhere exotic, by which I mean anywhere outside Nova Scotia. Being born and bred outside Nova Scotia has some kind of story attached. The woman in the obituary was carried here from Boston as a three-month-old infant. Why were they in Boston? Why did they move here so soon after the baby was born?

Maybe another came as a child through Pier 21, the immigration shed in Halifax Harbour through which over one million immigrants arrived in Canada between 1928 and 1971. Maybe adults from another hemisphere chose this tiny spot out of all the spots on the globe.

'Born and bred here' is what you say if your story isn't something else. Everyone starts somewhere.

Two people added 'Bluenoser' to 'born and bred' in the survey responses. Two in one hundred are the exceptions that prove the rule: we don't call ourselves Bluenosers much nowadays, at least not when we're home. It described early Nova Scotian sailors who were so cold their noses turned blue, or who ate blue potatoes with their salt herring. The famous racing schooner *Bluenose*, which was named for the people, not the other way around, still graces our dimes, and a replica of it sails for the provincial tourism department, but use of the term is mostly limited to names of events like the Blue Nose Marathon, held in springtime when runners' noses may turn as blue from cold as the sailors' noses did and still do.

What happens after we're born and raised in, or emigrate to, Nova Scotia? Must we remain on this sea-bound peninsula, while lobsters from our waters jet off to eager diners on the other side of the world, and pretty balsam fir trees decorate Christmases in the Caribbean? Do we break some loyalty code if we wander abroad ourselves, see the world a little?

We do wander, in droves. I don't know if other places are as painfully familiar with the phrase 'goin' down the road' as Nova Scotia is, but for decades, opportunities for education, work, or culture all seemed to be elsewhere, and the road sloped downhill toward them. But Nova Scotia's population has staged a recent turnaround, according to Statistics Canada. In 2000, the population was 933,821; on our way to 2010, the number rose and dipped and rose again to 942,107. In 2019, it topped the charts at 971,395. Reasons for growth include inter-provincial migration (more coming up the road than going down) and immigrants, including recent Syrian refugees. And we had more births than deaths – a very unusual change of affairs.

More born to be raised here. But will they stay?

There are a surprising number of ways to leave Nova Scotia, a peninsula with a narrow connection to the mainland. You can drive the Trans-Canada Highway (or take a bus or train) across the windy Tantramar Marshes on the Isthmus of Chignecto to New Brunswick and the rest of the Western Hemisphere.

You can fly from the R L Stanfield International Airport at Halifax to anywhere in the world, or from the J A Douglas McCurdy Sydney airport to destinations in Canada.

You can sail on the ferry from Digby to Saint John, New Brunswick. There was a ferry from Yarmouth to a port in Maine, and may be again, though the provincial government's spending millions of dollars on it doesn't guarantee that. And there's the ferry from Caribou to Wood Islands, Prince Edward Island, after which you can drive across the Confederation Bridge to New Brunswick. At the eastern end of Cape Breton, you can sail on ferries from North Sydney to Newfoundland ports, though not so many Nova Scotians go down that road; more likely the opposite.

Oddly, the great Port of Halifax is not a terminus for people travelling by water, other than for daily commuters crossing on the harbour ferries, or the thousands of tourists who arrive (with their dollars) for quick visits on giant cruise ships in summer, and the crews of Canada's naval ships, who leave for months at a time but return to great rejoicing.

Those navy boats don't bring passengers, but they do bring population. According to a government website, Nova Scotia is home to more than 40% of Canada's military assets. This includes this country's largest military base, CFB Halifax, which is the headquarters for Maritime Forces Atlantic. Other major military installations include 12 Wing Shearwater in Halifax Regional Municipality and CFB Greenwood in the Annapolis Valley. About ten thousand enlisted personnel call Halifax home, at least temporarily.

Driving across the Canso Causeway to Cape Breton Island from the mainland is not leaving Nova Scotia, though some Cape Bretoners insist it is. It counts as 'goin' down the road' only when you're southbound, leaving that island. That strong Cape Breton identity is legendary, and is known far beyond our border and shores – all the way down the road to Fort McMurray in Alberta, for instance, where many Cape Bretoners have gone to work in the oil patch. In fact, the identity is so strong that it is reported that people out there will buy ball caps only if they say Cape Breton on them. Nova Scotia caps don't sell well in Alberta.

Survey responses

Nova Scotia is where I began. My parents and grandparents, back many generations, began here. Home is where I married, had my children. There is a distinct connection to the land and the people, a sense of place and belonging. When we drive across the Tantramar Marshes, our hearts sing with joy, for this is OUR place, and the bond, although we have been "away," is strong.

<>

My husband's work and career in the military took us away for about twenty-three years. After leaving Nova Scotia I always knew I would return. Every time we crossed the New Brunswick border into Nova Scotia my heart and throat exploded with emotion. I was so happy to be home. [Now] I live on the family homestead my husband and I bought seventeen years ago.

Inbound traffic on all routes picks up in the summer, when tourists come to Nova Scotia for our scenery, fresh air, seafood, festivals, and our easy-going sensibilities. Embedded in those crowds are many born-and-breds coming home for a visit to the family homestead, a summer cottage, a beach rental, or a guest room with friends.

Another incoming population arriving late summer is transient but outsized. Nova Scotia boasts ten universities, and they attract a lot of students to our province from all over the world. Considering that there are just under one hundred colleges and universities in all of Canada, we're doing well. Our educators educate the world, and they do their darndest to encourage their graduates to make their homes here.

That sense of belonging which Jay LeBlanc experienced in Petit-Ruisseau is like a magnet for some. It can grip us tightly when we're within its field, which can extend over horizons. Magnets power our compasses, but if the swinging needle is not clearly marked we may be confused about which end points to home.

Jan Fancy Hull

Unfortunately, the magnet that pulls us sometimes gets turned around in the wrong hands, and may be used to repel little children like Vanessa Fells and her sister, skipping rope in the street outside their home in Yarmouth.

River Road
by Alex Hickey

My granddad fished
out in this bay
My mother packed fish
in the plant

Now all that's gone
And what remains
are widow walks
fresh painted by
"come from aways"

But the sky is the same
the same changeable
blue and clouds
same golden sun
shining red at day break
or when day is done

Each day I drive
The River Road to town
and work
glued to my desk and screen
and wonder if
this work will stay
while all around me
I see jobs evaporate

And each night I drive
the River Road
my heart in my mouth
just like Granddad said
he always felt
when he sailed south

And the sky is the same
the same changeable

blue and clouds
same golden sun
shining red at day break
and when day is done

My brother phones
from Edmonton
to tell me
life
is passing me by

"If you stay there
You'll never meet
An eligible guy.
You're getting older
And what will happen then,
If you've no kids? No man?"

But I fell in love
when I was just a girl
with waves that
foam and curl
and throw themselves
onto this sand
holding
nothing back
they hurl themselves
upon the mercy
of this land

And I am the same
the same changeable
blue and clouds
same golden sun
shining red at day break
and when day is done

Jan Fancy Hull

2 – Living the Dream

Survey responses

Home is the quiet solitude of the many beaches, the gurgle of the small brook that runs through my property.

<>

I was taken (by my husband) to Ontario for 25 years. I came home at least two times a year to see family. I am now back in Nova Scotia and I will never leave again. Ontario was kind to us but I pined for Nova Scotia every day. I missed the ocean. I am a fisherman's daughter and the sea is in my blood.

<>

I couldn't wait to move home while we were in Ontario...I needed my ocean.

<>

Living by the ocean is awesome.

Scenes and seasons

Pam Mood loves the salt water. "Growing up, I was always at the beach on weekends – and on Wednesday afternoons in those days, when town businesses used to take a mid-week break. If I lived elsewhere, I would never be able to get to the sea in two minutes like I can here. It means freedom. You really are on the edge of the world," she says. "Peace settles in my soul."

Pam can see the water through the windows of her office in Yarmouth's Town Hall, where she is serving her second term as Mayor of the town that adopted the brand *On the Edge of Everywhere*.

"Yarmouth is not at the end of the world," she says. "It's at the beginning. We are the welcome mat of the province. There's such a quality of life here. You can do anything here." Of course, it's her job to promote the town, but a short conversation soon shows her boosterism is genuine.

> *Survey response*
>
> *Nova Scotia has so much to see and do. We like camping. Some people like bar hopping lol but we love beach hopping and try to visit many different places throughout the summer. One of our favourites is Carter's Beach. The beaches and all the many campgrounds are our favourites. We love going to the many yard sales and mile long ones in the summer. I might add summer is my favourite season in NS. Road trips are the best.*
> *Also love taking the walk-on ferries to see other places you can't get to by car.*

On Cape Breton Island, Sandee MacLean, with her sister Heather Coulombe, owns The Farmer's Daughter Country Market in Whycocomagh (pop. 850), where you can buy baked goods, groceries, a souvenir Cape Breton ball cap, and so much more. In 2016, they posted a job offer on the market's Facebook page, offering not only employment in their enterprise, but two acres of land suitable for building a house on – free to the successful applicant who stays there five years.

They received thousands of responses and worldwide attention, and have made some successful hires as a result. "Some responders whom we hired didn't work out," Sandee told me. "They didn't get involved in the community on their own. They expected to be taken around and introduced. You can't feel welcomed in a community unless you get involved. Another couple we hired is totally integrated."

We are sitting at one of several shaded wooden picnic tables outside the Farmer's Daughter Market. A chattering group of Sandee's staff is gathering nearby, preparing to head out to a community fundraising event. Sandee gestures toward the group.

"See?" she says. "There's one of our new hires." I can't pick that person out from the others; all are talking and laughing together.

The Farmer's Daughter, ready to welcome you

"A lot of people who applied want stress-free lives," she says. "People have begun to value what we have here. No big mortgage, no long commute. Just friendly people, and nature, and a good job."

Sandee arrived at her perspective after much thought. "I always had the perfect house, wore make-up every time I left the house, my children were spending their time on the internet. I began to think, what values am I teaching my children? And here, you can see the stars."

She leads by example, too. "We're involved in volunteering; it's good for young people. But it should be fun, not a drag on their time." She observes that volunteer opportunities have changed from her childhood. "Church dinners are not so big now."

A passionate small-towner, Sandee says, "The kind of person I wanted was one who wants a simple life – but not easy. They'd have to work hard."

The land included in the deal had been in her family for generations. She and her sister worked to convince their father, who had owned the land with his father, of the wisdom of their scheme. Giving away land was an outlandish idea to him. "We own a lot of land," Sandee told me. "We wouldn't sell it, because it isn't that accessible [steep, no roads] and it would just be clear-cut."

If the prominent hillsides in Whycocomagh were clear-cut, I'm sure it would break Sandee's heart, and the hearts of many more. Scenery along the shores of the Bras d'Or Lake – the sparkling water, high hills or low mountains – is tourist-attracting and driver-distracting. The Bras d'Or is an inland lake of fresh and salt water, but it's not the sparkling water that especially appeals to Sandee. "It's the mountains for me. And the four seasons. Snowshoeing on the trail – I love to break the trail."

Sandee grew up in nearby Skye Glen on the family dairy farm, and now lives in Stewartdale, not far from there. "There are trails that run right behind the house, and mountains. I walk that trail four days a week, sort of a walking meditation, not thinking specifically about anything." That's where the idea to use land to turn new employees into neighbours popped into her head.

Survey response

I appreciate the scale of Halifax, the mix of old and new, the history, the diversity of people from all over the world, the presence of universities which adds to that diversity and culture. I value the very many different regions in our province. The south shore, the eastern shore, the Bay of Fundy – all have different features geologically speaking, and from the perspective of how the sea and the land meet. Cape Breton has its own characteristics topographically and culturally. I value the influence of the French and English settlers and the role that Nova Scotia played for the dispute between those two foreign powers as they tried for control over the new world (Halifax Citadel vs Louisbourg). I value the influence of Nova Scotia in other parts of the world: the Cajuns (Acadians) in Louisiana. I appreciate Halifax's role in World War Two as a safe harbour for convoys to marshal before heading to England with vital supplies. I value the role of the fishery in shaping the culture and even architecture (widow's walks in Lunenburg). I love the relatively slow pace of development in Nova Scotia, despite economic challenges. I love the neighbourhoods of Halifax and the sense of belonging in them. I value the ease of accessibility of Halifax, whether it is to culture or to the various relaxation places like the south shore or Annapolis Valley. I feel well in my skin when I am home. I feel my sense of place and where I fit in, historically speaking. I love the feeling of familiarity when I am home. I could go on.

Of course, Nova Scotia isn't all country trails and lighthouses. Nova Scotia has two cities: Halifax/Dartmouth (pop. 300,000) and Sydney (pop. 30,000). [Both cities are in regional municipalities which take in significant rural areas; I've included only their approximate urban populations here.]

Jan Fancy Hull

Jennifer Watts grew up in Halifax and now lives with her family there. With a background in community and urban development, she had 'gone down the road' to work in Nicaragua with CUSO; in Doha, Qatar; in Toronto; in Saskatoon. She came home again, served as a respected member of Halifax City Council, and now works as Executive Director of Immigrant Services Association of Nova Scotia (ISANS).

Why did she come back to Halifax? "Family. Ocean. The size of Halifax," she says.

We're meeting in the food court of a shopping mall near her office, a convenient stop on her way home after work. Jennifer leads a very busy life. I test her on the ocean reference. Many people say they love the ocean, but does she really take the time to go there? "No, I don't see the ocean a lot," she admits. "I might smell it, hear the fog horn, but it's important to me to know it's there."

It's there, all right. Even if you're far inland, when the wind is blowing onshore the ocean will remind you that it's there. The groaning of the whistle buoys marking shoals, fog horns on great ships in the harbours, the smell of seaweed tossed on the rocks, and the pervasive fog – these are reminders that we are nearly surrounded by the ocean and "on the edge of everywhere" as Pam Mood says Yarmouth is. And because of our peninsular shape, if you go more than sixty-five kilometres inland to retreat from the fog, you'll be heading out to the other side and toward the ocean again, somewhere along Nova Scotia's 7400 kilometres of rugged coastline.

Survey responses

I have to confess to avoiding parts of winter...
it is definitely too long.

<>

I am old enough to be thinking about my next chapter of senior
life. I would like to be by the Atlantic again, but I am not looking
forward to the winters. So I am stymied.

<>

I would love to [return to NS] except I am not used to harsh
winters anymore.

Oh come now, are the winters really so bad? Well, yes, they can be, depending on your age, health, attitude, and ability to get around in slush, snow, sleet, freezing rain...but don't take my word for it. What did Veryan Haysom think of winter weather in Nova Scotia when he first came here? Veryan was born in South Africa, a hot, bright country. Nova Scotia's "fabulously infamous miserable gray spring weather" almost sent him back there.

"I came to Cape Breton in December 1968 and did some work supply-teaching, some construction work on the family home we were building then. In the fall of 1969, I went to law school at Dalhousie in Halifax. That proved to be a very difficult year for me," Veryan recalls.

"The law courses themselves weren't what made it difficult. It was the whole experience of being in Halifax in a very demanding academic program, through the winter. I'd already had a winter in Cape Breton when I first arrived, so it wasn't a surprise, but it was the second winter when the beast finally landed. I found it grey, depressing, utterly unlike anything I'd experienced in South Africa to that point."

Perhaps Nova Scotians born and raised in this climate are advantaged in that we don't have the complication of comparing our drab seasons to a far, far, brighter place. Young Veryan was despondent and ready to abandon his studies in Halifax when some Canadian classmates befriended him and convinced him to stay another year.

"I can't say that I immediately thought, 'Isn't this wonderful!'" he says. "It didn't bring the sun out, but it was an introduction to characters who simply embraced the miserable weather, and revelled in it. I think that's a very Canadian sort of thing – the ability to just simply go out and enjoy the cold, the snow, winter sports, and beyond that, the ability to laugh in the face of rain, drizzle, fog, ice, sleet – and get on with the pleasures of life."

Veryan Haysom is still living in Nova Scotia, more than fifty winters and springs later.

Warm Winter Blues
by Janet Hull
Novascotian / Chronicle Herald February 2012

Winter makes me sick.

Yes, I know, you too. You have SAD, winter blahs, frost-bite, yellow-snow fever, and you're shack-wacky. I'm not. I wish I were.

I have a rare disease that destroys my red blood cells when the temperature turns cold. Not good to be outdoors in Nova Scotia's winter. So I'm taking refuge in a warmer clime. I have mixed feelings about this. I'm homesick for winter.

I miss that cosy denned-in feeling when the snow has drifted so high that I can't push my door open. I miss being unable to get my car out because my only neighbour with the plow thinks the crusty snow in the lane will melt soon anyway, and offers to bring me milk and bread from his freezer if I need them. Why else would I want to go out?

Instead, I'm keeping warm in Florida, where balmy breezes waft across the Gulf from Valhalla. Skies cloud over seldom, briefly. At home, if we have three straight days of good weather in any season we say "We'll pay for this." Down here, it's all reward and no pay for, this time of year anyway. It's hard to reconcile this style of winter with that of my home and native land, but I manage. Doctor's orders.

But when I'm reclining in my chair on a broad, white, sandy beach beneath a ten-mile-high sky, I recall falling backwards with complete trust into the arms of a white angel, winter's pale sun and five layers of clothing insulating me from the soft, cold snow.

People gather on these Gulf beaches just to watch the sun set in golden water. The warm sub-tropical night sky that follows is full of familiar stars, reminding me of the winter moon rising from behind the evergreens at the edge of my snowy fields at home. You can see for miles in that different darkness, as with lightning. The very air is dark blue and restorative to breathe.

Then you go inside and your glasses fog up and you drink something hot and sweet.

Yes, I know, not all days and nights in Maritime winters are sparkly. There are blizzards. Between them, temperatures moderate, dirty snow-banks leak fluid, clouds hang low overhead like grey wool blankets on the line threatening to pull it all down. This snowbird loves those shadow-less days when the sun seems neither to rise nor set, but for a few hours the street lights go out and soon come on and it is dark again. Those are special days. You may not even get dressed. You can feel melancholy and not have to explain why. Sunshine isn't everything. There's slush.

A 1978 song by Jesse Winchester nails it:

> *O that sad old wintry feeling*
> *I don't really seem to mind*
> *Sad but sweet old wintry feeling...*
> *somehow it just seems to suit me fine.*

Jan Fancy Hull

Anne Murray said her crew sometimes warmed up with that song before her shows, tuning their voices by singing that sweet old wintry feeling into them. What an iconic Canadian moment: our Anne singing – Look how the sky's all silver.../ and out of the sky of silver,/ snowflakes begin to fall.

I move that we adopt Wintry Feeling as our winter national anthem. Do I have a seconder?

Gilles Vigneault sang *Mon pays, ce n'est pas un pays, c'est l'hiver* [My country isn't a country, it's winter]. That can be our new pledge of allegiance; we'll share it with all nations around both poles. I would fervently pledge allegiance "to winter and the people upon which it descends, one nation, under snow." Even though I am forced into warm exile from it, can't make me say I don't love it.

In the Land of the Free, patriots hold their hand over their heart for their national anthem. I propose in the Land of the Freeze that we tuck both hands in our parka's armpits (or in the armpits of someone else's parka if invited) as we sing our winter anthem, softly stamping our feet, too, if we're outside or in a hockey rink. We'll sing it to each other lovingly wherever we gather, or tipsily as we leave your house after a winter party (someone else is driving).

We'll be warmer, giving ourselves – or sharing – a hug. We might feel a little melancholy as we sing. But we'll feel cosy, too, and closer to each other.

And that will cheer us up a lot.

My reference above to "paying for" the weather is a common expression and attitude in Nova Scotia. If we get an especially nice day or, more rare, a string of 'em, someone will say, "We'll pay for this!" I try not to say it myself; it's bad psychology to feel guilty for good weather, though I do know it won't last forever. That's the frequent conclusion to the conversation: "Yeah, well, wait five minutes and it'll change."

I found these statistics: foggy old Halifax receives some bright sunshine on at least 43% of the days in the year, and thereby is the sunniest place in Nova Scotia. On two hundred ninety days in the year, Halifax has some measurable sunshine, if only a momentary glimpse through the gloom. Surely, we wouldn't have to pay for those lucky flashes.

Nova Scotia isn't the only place in Canada with gorgeous scenery, or winters that bite. If you accept the premise that those playing fields are more or less level across the country, you might believe that you could attract a number of people to move from more populous regions to little Nova Scotia, where each new family creates a noticeable uptick in our prosperity. Sandee MacLean believed it, and it's working for her and her sister in Whycocomagh.

Survey response

I love Nova Scotia for being so close to the ocean and the beautiful scenery. I can walk along many trails and enjoy peace of mind and relaxation.

There are a lot of different-but-same conversations in this book. Many of us share similar feelings, but about different things. Or we feel differently about the same things. This may be our underlying unity: we want to be agreeable, and we have enough in common that we often seem to agree, even when we don't.

You may have been present when someone tells a story about, say, going to a restaurant, and another will say, "Exactly! That's like what happened to me..." and what comes next isn't the same at all, except both likely dined out somewhere. This does challenge newcomers whose thoughts may follow different neural paths; more about our language quirks in another chapter.

In that context, I want to add one of those 'that's like this' comments to Yarmouth's claim to being *On the Edge of Everywhere*. At the opposite end of the Nova Scotian mainland is the community of Canso (population 750 or so). Canso figured large in several major events since 1604, but its fortunes faded in recent decades, with the against-all-odds exception of the Stan Rogers Festival that attracts ten thousand music-lovers each summer.

Canso is at the end of a long road, not on the way to anywhere except the North Atlantic Ocean. That's why Canso caught the attention of an enterprise which is preparing to build a commercial spaceport just outside town. Against all odds, being at the back of beyond and 'on the edge of nowhere' may turn out to be Canso's 21st century cash crop, if the environmental risks and intermittent but spectacular disturbances of the peace from rockets blasting off are acceptable to the residents.

Canso and Yarmouth somehow share similarities, if only for the ways they differ.

Culture and coffee

Some enterprising business owners and community leaders in Lunenburg County shared The Farmer's Daughter's beliefs and put their beliefs in motion – literally. They sponsored a retro Boler trailer covered in bright graphics, pulled by an SUV, driven by a very enthusiastic ambassador for the county. Their organization, "NOW Lunenburg County", sent Tina Hennigar and her rig across the country in 2017 to engage in conversations with people of all kinds about what Lunenburg County had to offer. What does it offer? Picturesque fishing villages? Maple syrup? Lobster? What was the value proposition she towed across seven provincial borders?

"Other places are beautiful, too," Tina agrees. "In Whistler, British Columbia, everything – and everyone – is gorgeous. But nobody there made eye contact. I went out across Canada to sell the beauty of this place, but changed over to the beauty of our people, who are incredibly extraordinary." Tina's eyes well up with emotion at the thought. "I couldn't wait to come back home. In some places the people were pretentious, or exclusive, and I wondered: what is the vibe we give off when people come here?"

It takes guts to drive into other communities saying 'Come down east 'cause our people are really nice,' but Tina pulled it off. "Some people asked me what I was offering as an incentive to move east. I told them I'm offering the opportunity to affect your community, to make a difference – not like Vancouver where nobody knows you."

Survey response

Other than my house and gardens, this has never felt like home. When I go away for extended periods of time I never long to be back here and never miss it. I never realized how much I would love a large city, Vancouver in particular, until our youngest son moved there in 2010. I have spent time there in every season and spent three months there last year.
Did I miss the Maritimes or [this town]? Not even for a second of the entire time I was there. I now have more real friends there than I do here. I find the people far friendlier; shop-keepers remember me from visit to visit.

Chacun à son goût. That survey response shouldn't be a surprise, really – at least not the part about liking Vancouver. Six hundred and forty-eight thousand people live in Vancouver City proper, so one assumes that many of them like living there, maybe even as much as that person likes to visit.

A few dozen people who may not love the big city as much wouldn't be missed, and NOW Lunenburg County or Cape Breton or any other region of Nova Scotia would be thrilled to have that many newcomers make their home here.

Population is a critical factor in our small, rural economies: a family brings children for the schools, workers or employers for enterprises, customers for vendors, occupants for homes, cultural variety, skills, taxes for government services, and new neighbours who want to contribute to their community. A dwindling population loses all that.

"We don't offer big pay in Nova Scotia," Tina Hennigar told those who stopped to see what her bright caravan was all about. "Money is secondary; enjoyment of life is important. People asked if we're having a financial boom. I told them we're having a lifestyle boom!"

Sandee MacLean in Whycocomagh would agree with Tina. "I wasn't hiring employees," she says. "I was building the community."

The incentive of two acres of land is, in Sandee's view, of lesser value than the opportunity to live an enriched life in a quality community. It did grab worldwide attention, however.

It's natural that people would pay more attention if a "hook" is attached to a soft concept, though. Nova Scotian communities have plenty of unused land that they could offer to deserving newcomers. The Farmer's Daughter proved that potential new residents find it intriguing to earn a few acres just by coming here and helping to build the community in which they will live.

Survey response

The scenery, talent, music and friendliness in Nova Scotia, and more specifically, Cape Breton, is second to none.

Of the twenty-eight people I interviewed for this book, about half happen to be practitioners of arts and crafts in varying degrees: a pewter Christmas ornaments designer, a writer, a rug hooker, a quilt art maker, a stained glass maker, a wooden signs maker, a church pianist, a milliner, a painter, a choir conductor, and a drag performer / visual artist...and I carve stone.

Nova Scotia tourism advertising promotes our dancing and fiddle-playing and lobsters boiling on the beach. Popular music thrives in Nova Scotia, with many performers making solid careers. We send top classical performers to the world's stages as well; and though our own stages are small, some top performers do come back here, at least on tour.

One who does come back, and brings her world-class performing group with her, is Lydia Adams, conductor of the Elmer

Iseler Singers, a busy, twenty-voice professional choir based in Toronto. She's a native of Glace Bay (pop. 19,000), and credits that coal-mining town with giving her what it took to get her start.

"Cape Breton and my mother started it – the love of music, learning to not be rattled when things went wrong, to just go around it. It became like breathing. If I hadn't grown up in that environment, I wouldn't have been able to go forward, aiming for the highest level."

How did she feel, leaving the home she loved to pursue her career? "Opportunities for me are where the great choirs are, in Toronto, or London, England, for instance. You go to see everything there, every day, twice a day; you soak up great, great art. That's just not readily available in a smaller place, nor therefore is the possibility to make a living at it. Also, the body of singers to work with at the highest level is only available in a larger centre. But my home made it possible for me to start out and achieve my goals."

Lydia Adams' busy work life doesn't permit her to spend a lot of time in her house outside of Toronto "where I live," but she does enjoy a virtual community with long-time friends from back home. "We often connect in emails or texts. One of us might notice an item in the Cape Breton *Post* [newspaper] about something or someone we all know about, and a conversation will start up. We're a close-knit group, also all professional musicians, and we share the same sense of humour."

Similar to Vanessa Fells, whose larger home is the Black community, Lydia has a home she carries in her heart. "Because of the work I'm in, creating beautiful music with singers is one of my homes," she says. When her choirs travel to perform and present workshops in cities and remote communities across Canada, it's Lydia who works to ensure the experience is welcoming for her audience and participants.

"I've been a newcomer to communities all over the country, on stage. We've visited high schools, First Nations communities, churches, synagogues. It's always a thrill to share great music. Even if someone has a small voice, that's fine; a small voice gets put together with other voices. It's wonderful, in choirs, how you can be part of something that is much greater than yourself. That's a real community experience."

She tells me proudly that there are three and a half million choral singers in Canada, according to a recent census: that's ten percent of Canada's population, breathing together, singing together.

Nova Scotia has symphony orchestras; professional theatres; art galleries; festivals everywhere of all sorts; concert series in churches, barns, old schools, and stages in fields – all doing their best to entertain us with their performances, toe-tapping or otherwise. And there is usually some fine food available nearby before or after the show, though the picturesque lobsters-on-the-beach scenario may be somewhat over-sold by tourism promoters.

Sometimes it rains. Bring rain gear, warm clothing, sunscreen, bug spray....

Lydia makes pilgrimages home to Cape Breton as often as she can. In the summer of 2017, she brought her professional choir to Lunenburg, Baddeck, and Halifax. The choir's special guest in Baddeck was Canada's first female astronaut, Roberta Bondar. Adams had composed a multi-media choral work in celebration of the astronaut's trip into space. Since 2017 was the twenty-fifth anniversary of that voyage, they toured it 'down east,' including at the Bell Museum in Baddeck, the birthplace of flight in Canada.

"It's so great to bring great music home," Lydia says. "It's coming full circle for me." While many in the audience stayed after that concert to greet the astronaut, who is a captivating speaker, the home-town people lining up to greet Lydia Adams were also star-struck.

Survey response

Nova Scotia is a beautiful place with so much to offer and so much talent musically.

Cultural experiences do matter, not only to current residents, but also to those who are considering visiting or moving here. Scenery doesn't entertain after the sun goes down, (though a few survey respondents mentioned the night sky) or when the fog rolls in.

If you Google "Vancouver", for example, this may pop up in the corner of your screen:

> Vancouver, a bustling west coast seaport in British Columbia, is among Canada's densest, most ethnically diverse cities. A popular filming location, it's surrounded by mountains, and also has thriving art, theatre and music scenes. Vancouver Art Gallery is known for its works by regional artists, while the Museum of Anthropology houses preeminent First Nations collections.

Do you notice that? Of all that Vancouver offers, the banner attractions are cultural: filming, art, theatre, music, artists, and museums. With diversity and mountains. There's hardly a mention of industry, other than the bustling seaport, and nothing about minimum wage or the hellish cost of living.

So Sandee MacLean and Tina Hennigar are not wrong to stake their campaigns to attract newcomers on lifestyle. Cultural life matters everywhere, and we have lots of it in Nova Scotia to feel at home with. People who establish businesses or get jobs and move here want to know what's there to do after work. Collectively, cultural aspects help make up what's considered quality of life, an important component of feeling at home.

Coffee-shops are homey-feeling places, too, if they do it right. In some communities, they are the unofficial town square. I have a theory about small town cafés: if there's a Tim Horton's or McDonald's in your community, you've achieved a kind of critical mass, with enough population or traffic to warrant the investment (Tim's franchisees need at least $1.5 million in net worth to start). Having one of those franchises in your town is just a basic, like a grocery store, pharmacy, or bank.

But if you also have an indie café and roastery in an old building with parking on the street and no drive-thru, that's a step up, a sign that there are people in your town earning enough money to fork out the higher prices for a specialty coffee made by a barista. Good to have both.

<blockquote>

Survey response

Nova Scotia is peaceful and has a good variety of the arts to enjoy.

</blockquote>

Even our larger communities need new residents, and they need them to integrate. "Lots of people are buying up old homes in town, and that's nice to see," says Deanne Fitzpatrick of Amherst (pop. 9,413), where she teaches rug hooking and creates hooked art in her studio, a pilgrimage destination for fibre artists.

"Some do get involved. Amherst is an easy community to get involved in – but you do have to leave your house and join in: golf, curling, churches, book clubs, Tai Chi, YMCA, library – and rug hooking."

I ask Mayor Pam Mood about young people 'goin' down the road' out of Yarmouth. She responds, "Many of our youth have gone away, and I say, let them. They need to see the world. But now, they're returning, so how do we help them fit in?"

It's not an idle question: as Mayor, it's her job to come up with answers to it.

Pam agrees with me about cafés and the like. "We are attracting doctors and pharmacists and lawyers, but also food trucks and craft beer, and we'll do anything to promote them. If people are going to move here, or move back here, you have to have the amenities that will attract and hold them, even including fresh paint on buildings, pedestrian-friendly bump-outs on the streets. They can't argue with the cost of living here, nor with the quality of life."

In an imaginary café, I see Pam Mood, Tina Hennigar, and Sandee MacLean seated at a table, exclaiming "Yes!" to each other.

Pull up another chair to that café table: here comes Annette Verschuren. Annette has had a remarkable business career – which is far from over. The former CEO of Home Depot Canada, she writes with delightful candour about it in her book, *Bet On Me*. She remains committed to Cape Breton and the community where she began, on her family's dairy farm near North Sydney (pop. 6,000).

"I wish the government would work to keep its successful sons and daughters connected to the province in some way," Annette says. "That's the recipe for constructing an attractive community."

Note that she didn't say to keep our sons and daughters in the province; rather, keep them connected to it. So they'll return, as Pam Mood says. As for herself, Annette Verschuren says, "I never left." Though she "needed to" live and work in Toronto to fulfill her ambitions, as did Glace Bay's Lydia Adams, Annette keeps a log home, a condo, a dairy farm, and her heart, in Cape Breton.

In 2018 I happened to glimpse a TV news item about the North American Free Trade Agreement (NAFTA) negotiations. In the lineup behind the federal Minister in charge of negotiations was Annette Verschuren.

Annette and I are sitting on a bench on the porch of our Baddeck hotel, the fragrant morning air freshened by a rollicking electrical storm the night before. It's a lovely setting for talk about how Nova Scotia can be a more attractive home for its people. "Our small communities need to have high-speed internet," Annette told me. "Cafés serving cappuccinos. Restaurants offering local food. Stores selling local produce and goods. Artists and the arts. Small businesses, no copy-cat stores."

I'm familiar with a couple of towns that offer much of that. She's right: they are doing well, and they're very attractive to live in or visit. "Nova Scotia should stop thinking about attracting big business," she continues. "Tourism and agriculture should be our main focus. And expand tourism in winter – snow is an asset."

Sure, snow is inconvenient and costs money: home heating, plowing, salting, lost work days, power outages, coats, and slush-repelling boots, none of which comes as an option or with a subsidy. But snow can also make money: downhill and cross-country skiing, snowmobile trails, snow-shoeing, outdoor adventures, winter festivals, all have their followers who need hot and cold beverages, dry socks, food, lodging, and transportation.

As I was writing this, I saw a news report that Tourism Cape Breton had launched a new promotion of winter activities. Annette would approve.

Sandee MacLean agrees with Annette Verschuren and Pam Mood about community development. "A call centre is not the way," Sandee says. "The government should give payroll rebates to small businesses to help them grow, and grow their communities. Why not promote mentoring? A meat cutter at the local Co-op store here in Whycocomagh was trained by local employers. Some of our employees were not succeeding at front-of-store jobs, so we moved them to the bakery, where they are learning and succeeding."

"Confidence is key," Annette Verschuren says, and she exhibits plenty of that, as do the others around my imaginary café table. It wasn't handed to her: she worked hard for everything she has. Her parents came to Nova Scotia from the Netherlands along with fifty other Dutch families in the fifties.

"I'm the Dutchman's daughter," she says. "I'm a first generation Dutch Canadian from Cape Breton, and I've kept my Dutch heritage. They used to call my parents DPs – Depend on Parliament – though they never received any government money. I spent the first thirty years of my life working in Nova Scotia. I was driven by my career ambitions to make money. After working in Sydney, I considered Halifax, but didn't see anything there. I needed to go to Toronto to fulfill my ambitions."

NOW Lunenburg County's "lifestyle boom" would not provide a strong enough attraction to keep Annette here for work; it's not for everyone. "I still feel I live here, though admittedly, not full time," she says. "I love Toronto and Ontario, but I want to be buried in Cape Breton."

Not yet, please; Annette is very much alive, engaged in a new forward-looking enterprise, and supporting her home province. "Nova Scotia hasn't lost me. I've invested lots in the province, through the Verschuren Centre at the University of Cape Breton [where she is Chancellor], for example."

After I returned home from Baddeck, Annette emailed: "We discovered a great place for cappuccinos downtown!" I passed her recommendation on to other friends who visited there later in the summer; they enjoyed their coffees so much that they intended to go back again. Such amenities are a draw, and can make a town feel like home.

Safe haven

> *Survey response*
>
> *My husband and son are here in NB and we built our house here so I will likely never leave. Nova Scotia is the province I would go to if some sort of major life-alteration occurred (zombie apocalypse).*

When I raise the question about moving away, some people I interviewed admitted that, yes, they did move away once – meaning to another town within Nova Scotia or just a few miles across our border into New Brunswick – not exactly far 'away,' but it is indicative of how attached some Nova Scotians are to their hometowns. Pam Mood says she moved away from Yarmouth – to Wolfville, to get a degree in Political Science, and to Halifax for a Business Certificate.

Deanne Fitzpatrick in Amherst says she has no plans to move away, "but if there was some extreme life change, I might move to Sackville, NB." That's a distance of eighteen kilometres across the Tantramar Marsh. Perhaps she and the survey respondent quoted above would cross paths as they fled from the zombies.

Well, which way would you run?

There is a Nova Scotian connection to zombies, sort of. Just joking, I mentioned the survey comment about the zombie apocalypse to Vanessa Fells, who thought it might be a reference to the 2013 Brad Pitt movie, *World War Z*. She had watched it with her family at home in Yarmouth, and recalled laughing at the part about the zombie refugee camp at Freeport on Digby Neck. It's not far from Yarmouth as the crow flies, but travelling on the road to Freeport (pop. 223) involves 157 kilometres of scenic drive to the end of Digby Neck on Long Island – a perfect refuge from critters that would eat your brains, as residents know and visitors discover.

Freeport as she is

I watched the movie, purely for research, you understand. Sure enough, Pitt's movie family is sent to Freeport for their protection from the 'zombie pandemic.' I noted three fake news details in their heartwarming Freeport reunion scene: the perfect little harbour isn't actually Freeport (a cove in England plays the part), everyone in the camp is wearing a parka but it's not winter, and there's a US warship outside the harbour.

Freeport as Hollywood sees her

I know that third detail would never happen. Why? In January 2017, while huge crowds of women were marching in Washington DC and other cities around the globe to protest deplorable attitudes espoused by the new US President, fifteen women from Sandy Cove, population sixty-five, also marched. *Fifteen*. These women, some wearing parkas, some with iconic pink tuques, marched to declare what they will and will not stand for in their community: they will not stand for violence against women. Each year since then, more marchers have joined them to quadruple their numbers, some coming from as far away as Halifax.

As you must pass through Sandy Cove to get to Freeport, I'd trust the women of Sandy Cove to easily repel any zombies. Foreign warships not required.

That 'little march that roared' received world-wide attention from other marches, and locally from the Nova Scotia Museum of Natural History, which immediately obtained six of the Sandy Cove protest signs for its permanent collection.

I love that they are now part of our heritage, too.

Just a sidebar to the zombie topic, and then I'm done, I promise. If you search around the internet, you may find attempts to dehumanize and demonize migrants and refugees by describing them as zombies. Our initial response to both seems to be to repel, drive back, and destroy. Is this good food for thought? Fictional action movies may help us understand our response to a very real human tragedy. Contrast and compare.

Our Paradise
By Michelle Greek, on her Greatideamomy blog in 2016

If you've ever wondered where the best place to live is, I have the answer. It's Barss Corner, Nova Scotia. There's no doubt in my mind.

We bought our house on June 1st 2015, moving only 5 km down the road from our previous house in New Germany. Big changes happened with 5km!

It has been 15 months of Barss Corner living. Things are different here. Many times I have come home to a delivery on our doorstep. Some days it's a freshly baked apple pie. Sometimes it's homemade jams. Sometimes it's freshly squeezed juices. Sometimes it's homemade bread. Twice it has been fresh fish. Many days there have been veggies. Today I came home to three zucchinis, three green peppers, a large collection of peas, many cherry tomatoes and a jar of zucchini relish sitting on our step. Sometimes I figure out where the gifts come from, other times it remains a mystery. Today's gift is a mystery.

The chickens who lay the eggs we eat for breakfast and the cows who become our beef can be heard from our yard in the evenings.

We can bike to the store, where we are on a first name basis with all of the staff; where we can play a game of checkers; where we can borrow a book from the Little Library.

My children go by themselves to the post office to check our mail and come home with stickers and snacks.

We walk to church on Sunday mornings.

We spend Tuesday mornings exploring a neighbour's beautiful garden with many other neighbourhood children.

Sunday evenings involve a saxophone club and Thursday evenings have often been neighbourhood sewing evenings.

In the mornings, after breakfast, my children go outside and yell to their friends "It's time to play!"

At suppertime, I open our back door and call for my children to come inside to eat.

When I go for bike rides and walks with my children, others automatically join us. A friendly honk and wave comes from nearly every tractor, truck, and car who meet us on the road.

We are surrounded by ponds, streams and fields where we watch animals live and grow.

We pick berries and apples from fields and orchards that are within walking distance of our home, some being in our own back yard. We watch our vegetables grow from seeds.

There are hills for spending winter afternoons sledding down. And a friendly neighbour always seems to help when it's time to shovel.

Some days when we arrive home from outings, there are children in our yard, waiting to play.

We eat a meal with neighbours at least once a week.

A perfect little park for swimming and playing sits on a nearby lake. And I hear there is a hidden outdoor recreation gem sitting even closer to us, waiting for us to explore this fall.

The people are friendly. The scenery is beautiful. The discoveries are endless. It is a welcoming environment.

There is no other place I would rather raise my children than right here in Barss Corner. It is the best place to live.

3 – New Here vs From Here

Survey responses

Been in NS for 6 summers. Being called a CFA can be tiring at first. But once you are accepted you are in for good.

<>

At first I was called a CFA...didn't even know what that was. Soon after moving here...I was delighted when someone thought that I was a Nova Scotian. Indeed a compliment!

<>

We have new people in our community of thirteen houses. We have spoken on a number of occasions, when walking our respective dogs, but they seem to value their privacy and haven't socialized with us at our neighbourhood functions as of yet. We were welcomed into our community and have integrated well. It's fantastic to have such wonderful neighbours who have been there to offer help and advice whenever it's been needed. We really are very lucky!

<>

The day we moved into our house in December 1985 with a baby in my arms my neighbour said as she was going from her car to her house, "It's a hell of a time to be moving." That was the last I heard from her for many, many months, and indicative of how unwelcoming this community was.

<>

Nova Scotia is my (adopted) home. It is where my real family is, not the one I was born with.

<>

When we moved into the community, not one person came up to our home to welcome us. I was a bit shocked as Nova Scotians promote themselves as so welcoming! Not the case: not one casserole or cake received!

Welcome gifts

Wouldn't you expect, four centuries or more after settling on (or invading) these shores, that we'd have figured out how to welcome and integrate other movers-in who came later?

We need more people to fill our schools and pay taxes to pave our roads – welcome!

We need diverse cultures to enrich us with their fashions and cuisine and perspectives – welcome!

We need people to create enterprises to employ those of us who are loath to move away – welcome!

In theory, we do want that. Government wants it, business wants it, education, health care, every institution wants it. But there remains an undercurrent of exclusionary acronyms: CFA, but NIMBY: Come From Away, but Not In My Back Yard. Some folk strenuously object to the term Come From Away, even though there's a happy, award-winning, Broadway musical (about events in Newfoundland and Labrador) by that title.

Pam Mood feels that calling someone a CFA is "ugly and derogatory," but perhaps it's all in how it's said. Many survey respondents used the term, mostly not as a pejorative, and I've used it in this book as I received it.

Some newcomers to a community call themselves CBC, meaning Come By Choice, but people who work with immigrating newcomers just call them new Canadians, or our new friends, which eliminates the judgmental labels.

That last survey responder I quoted expected a cake or casserole (or a welcome) and was disappointed that they were never delivered. I'm curious: did we ever do that, or is it a myth?

If we know they're coming, as the 1950 song goes, do we bake a cake?

"People don't cook as much now, fewer people bake pies. Maybe that's it," Phyllis Price suggests. I'm having tea with her and her husband, Eric Hustvedt, in Broad Cove (pop. 125) at the kitchen table they have shared for four decades. "People did take food to a neighbour after his wife died," Eric suggests. "But that was in response to a perceived need, not as a welcoming gift."

Lydia Adams recalls hearing stories of people sharing food when it was desperately needed in Glace Bay. "Before my time, things were very, very tough. There's a story that soup bones made the rounds of the community, so everyone could have soup. Perhaps it's true."

She adds, "My grandparents would have lost their home at one time, had a Jewish man not helped them out. People don't forget these gifts. They have long memories. "

At the opposite end of the province, it was newcomers who fed the residents when supplies were scarce. "My great-grandfather came from Lebanon," Pam Mood says, "and Lebanese people serve. My grandfather, Fred Emin Sr., was Mayor of Yarmouth before me and I'm proud to say I'm a Yarmouthian of Lebanese descent. Here, I have the ability to walk down the street and know everyone – or I should. I love that people know my family before me. It's all connected." Her family owned a grocery store, and they were known to send out groceries at no charge when neighbours needed food.

Eric Hustvedt and Phyllis Price tell me a food story about a family from Syria who moved to a nearby village. The children were in school and doing okay, but language was a problem for their elders. Food is a common denominator anywhere, so "when they first arrived, they were invited to an event at the community hall – it was a Robbie Burns dinner! What must they have thought, to be presented with haggis!"

A classic casserole of the myth/expectation might have been made with Kraft dinner, canned tuna, canned cream of mushroom soup, canned peas, a dollop of mayonnaise – perhaps no more appealing than haggis to many new (or old) Nova Scotians. I have no idea how that fits into today's array of dietary choices, but I'm guessing it often doesn't. Such casseroles were a staple of church dinners when I was growing up, when homemakers mixed together everything that Kraft and Campbell's made, sometimes topped with bubbling Velveeta cheese or a scattering of corn flakes. You don't see casseroles like that served much now, though the recipes are still available online.

Survey response

> *We once were new people, now we are old people. Those who come here and wish to be social have no difficulty doing so.*

Eric and Phyllis are elders in Broad Cove now; Eric is north of seventy. They arrived in their twenties, he from the suburbs of Washington, DC and other US cities, she from Ontario. Their daughter and her husband now live just around the corner from them. Phyllis' mother has moved to nearby Liverpool.

"I always said that Broad Cove has good feng shui," Phyllis says. "I thought I would be in a fish bowl here, but no; it's nice to know somebody has your back." Eric agrees: "When our daughter was growing up here, someone always knew where she was if we didn't."

When newcomers arrive in the cove, they'll consider Eric and Phyllis as the establishment, and they'll find them welcoming.

Survey response

> *There are younger newcomers/families re-settling on older properties with their young growing families and adding a new vibrancy and hope for a more diverse, but vital, re-discovery of what it means to be a community & neighbours. They have actively introduced themselves. I immediately fell in love with them and see extensions of this interaction in the future.*

They might also find them suggesting things to do. "The Community Association has a program: when there are new people in the village, we go meet them, take a brochure about what's going on," Phyllis says. "We say they don't have to get involved – though that's not entirely true. We do want them to be involved."

Eric Hustvedt is a third-term Councillor for the Municipality of the District of Lunenburg (MODL), so it's his business to know and be known by his neighbours in Broad Cove and beyond. You'd expect him to knock on your door, and show up at as many church and community events as he can, it being more efficient to attend an event than to call a meeting.

Eric's district boundaries were altered significantly before an election, when the Municipality reduced the number of councillors from twelve to ten. "My district lost some home neighbourhoods, and added new ones where I wasn't known. Issues still come to me from the former districts even though they're now someone else's responsibility. And in the new ones, some people are surprised to learn that I'm now their councillor, even though I attend so many events there."

And even though they voted for him, presumably. Things do change, but slowly.

But here's a paradox: while some old ways are held onto, perhaps to the detriment of the hangers-on, some new ways can't come soon enough. "Rural broadband service is a priority, as identified by our constituents," Eric says. "I've been very involved in this initiative. Reason number one: the people want it. Reason number two: it's an economic development driver. A developer won't create a housing development [new homes for new residents] if there isn't internet access, because the houses won't sell."

Annette Verschuren would be shaking hands in agreement with Eric on that topic.

"Cell phone coverage is a priority also," Eric says. I can relate. Can you hear me now? is a frequent part of cell-phone conversations at my rural home. Eric says these tools of modern life are at least as important as good roads. "Maybe more so: we want fast internet and picturesque roads."

> *Survey responses*
>
> *Our neighbour is a hunter-gatherer so is often bringing us meat of one kind or other. He and his wife are good people and so are their children who live near us. Shortly after we moved here, there was White Juan [a hurricane-strength blizzard in February 2004, five months after a direct hit from Hurricane Juan]. Even though they didn't know us, a couple of neighbours called to see if we needed anything; one even snow-shoed back to see if we were okay.*
>
> <>
>
> *We all look out for one another the "country way." Not pop in all the time, but aware of what's going on along the road, offer or ask for help if necessary.*

If disaster strikes in Nova Scotia, such as a forest fire, or an airliner crashing into the sea, or a hurricane, or shipwreck, or a blizzard of epic proportions – all of which have happened here – just watch us jump into action. Nova Scotians have performed heroically and generously in those times, and always will.

In Petit-Ruisseau, Jay Leblanc's centuries-old family home once caught on fire. "My whole family moved in with the neighbours," she recalls, "who gave us shelter and food until we could move back home."

Could it be that refugees, who arrive with little or nothing after escaping from disaster, appeal to that same famous willingness to help in times of trouble?

On the other hand, do we assume that people who Come By Choice, and shell out big dollars to buy homes the locals can't afford, are self-sufficient and wouldn't need muffins or want a word of welcome from us?

Jan Fancy Hull

Code language

Survey response

I get along very well. One thing I found is people will find "easy" conversations, subjects they are familiar with. Often the outsider is unfamiliar with the subject and gets left out. But that's not unique to NS.

Surely the desire of every newcomer is to blend in, not to stick out as the newbie in new surroundings. As tourists abroad, we are advised not to dress or do things in a way that would alert locals to the fact that we don't know our way around.

Even for someone experienced at being a newcomer and who is invited here by locals, integrating into Nova Scotian life isn't easy, and one may find oneself sticking out in embarrassing ways. Krishna (Kris) Srivatsa has stories about that. He grew up in Mumbai, but he now says he's from Nova Scotia, even when visiting back in India.

"When I came first to Nova Scotia, to Truro, I got the job by phone, and was given the first seventeen nights' accommodation at the Holiday Inn. I had no idea what to expect. I had only my cat. It was my first time in Canada at all. 'Truro Heights' sounded good so I took a duplex there. But the neighbours were fighting and their semi-truck was noisy, so a year later I found another place. A [national] furniture store refused me credit; I never shop there now."

Dr. Srivatsa is an ICU physician in the hospital in Truro: I can't imagine that it was his ability to pay for a sofa that concerned that furniture shop's credit department.

Then there was the language barrier. Kris understands and speaks English fluently, with a slight musical accent on some words. But even after studying for a decade in the United States, he was puzzled by some Nova Scotian expressions.

"People at work here would ask me, 'How're you making out?' I had no idea what they meant. In the US, 'making out' means sticking your tongue in someone's mouth...so I said, 'Okaaay, I guess...' But I got used to Canadian ways, which are not the same as US ways."

A wedding is a happy event, most times, when two people vow to, among other things, make a home together. When Kris Srivatsa announced his wedding in 2016, his family was "all over it." As is the custom in India, twenty-five of his friends and family started the celebrations some days before the event at the "wedding house," a three-storey house he keeps with his partner in Halifax. Everyone happily shared the two bathrooms, much cooking, and "lots of air mattresses."

The wedding was conducted by Kris' father, a wedding officiant, who modified the traditional Hindu ceremony to apply to two grooms.

Meanwhile, the Nova Scotian family of Kris's new spouse, Brandt Eisner, almost didn't show up for the wedding. They had been acting distant since Brandt had come out. Brandt describes his parents as "very religious, so they have their issues with my lifestyle, though they've been better since the wedding. I was a 'good Christian boy' until age twenty-four. When I came out, I really came out. My parents struggled, but it's okay now. The wedding changed everything, though my parents didn't come for any events other than the wedding."

Home and community are complex topics with Kris and Brandt. We're in that very same Halifax wedding house for our interview. Though it isn't their primary residence, Kris feels very much at home in it, as though he lived there in a previous life. This belief was reinforced by a series of serendipities that made the house available for purchase just moments before they would have committed to buying another one they didn't like as well.

Brandt likes to think that living in India, where he has visited, would feel natural and exciting. Kris lived in India until he was twenty-three, and finds it to be behind the times in some ways. Kris moved around a lot in the last decade, and enjoys being settled in Nova Scotia now, though he says, "I've had offers from other provinces: less work, better pay. The current climate for physicians in Nova Scotia is not welcoming. But I don't want to move farther away from Boston, because my little niece is there."

Don't expect to see this couple chilling at a block party in Halifax or Truro. "Being a doctor," Kris explains, "people often try to ask me about their medical issues, but I have to avoid sidewalk diagnoses."

Brandt adds, "We talk to our neighbours, we say hi, but we don't hang out. Socializing has always been challenging for me; I don't do small talk. I think I got that from my mother. When she went out, she had an agenda, and would avoid stopping to talk with someone she knew to prevent being delayed. I can turn into that person, depending on which group is present." Brandt is an active and popular visual artist and gallerist. He is also a talented drag performer, turning himself into many people on stage.

Do you experience discrimination in your community or at work, either for brown skin or being gay, I ask Kris. "I prefer to keep a low profile," he says, "to prevent boundaries cropping up between me and my patients. There is homophobia in medicine; it was not good in Alabama where I did my residency – lots of jokes and insinuations. Not in Canada. There's a genuine openness here. Colour-blindness is a thing here, too. Nobody says anything."

When Kris, a good-looking and friendly single physician, first came to Truro, hospital staff were eager to suggest women for him to date. He eventually felt he had to set the record straight as to his preference. From then on, they suggested men.

Survey response

I am interested in genealogy, and know most of us are newcomers, so I have never really warmed to the idea of some community members being different.

Young Dalhousie law student Veryan Haysom, shoes soaked with slush, also had difficulty understanding a language he thought he knew as a South African. "It wasn't just the weather, to be honest. I also found Canadian society quite puzzling. I don't notice it as much now as I did then, but it was almost impossible to carry on a conversation with Canadians, or to begin a conversation with them, unless you were watching the same TV programs as they were. I'd grown up without TV. I was a twenty-year-old, devoid of the cultural context that everyone was taking for granted," he recalls. "At that time, they were actually revelling in it. Obviously, I didn't know anything about Canada, really, so all the cultural context was completely new to me."

"I think it was more difficult because, on the surface, there was so little difference. I, too, had come from a WASP background; we just didn't name it that way. We superficially spoke the same language, you know, studied the same literature. You would think you'd fit into the society very easily. And you have the illusion that that's the case. But the values and the assumptions and the context are very different."

Veryan says his struggle to fit in felt something like walking on uneven ground. "If there's a big step in front of you, you register it, and take the step. But if it's a tiny little step you may simply mis-judge it and get quite a jolt. It's almost surrealistic when you recognize all the images but they're just not going together right."

It's hard not to speak in code if you're unaware you're doing it. A former colleague who moved from Ottawa to Halifax had purchased a house, and was telling me where her street joined a main thoroughfare.

"It's near the Blockbuster store," she said.

"Oh," I said, "you mean where the liquor store used to be?"

"What is it with you people," she exclaimed, "always referring to places and things that used to be there? How can I navigate with landmarks that no longer exist, or are known by nicknames?"

Fair point. Consider the two bridges that span Halifax Harbour. One is known to locals as the old bridge, the other as the new bridge. The Angus L MacDonald, the old, was opened in 1955; the

A Murray MacKay, the new, in 1970. Both are old bridges now, though the MacDonald underwent a 'big lift' refit recently, making it newer in some parts.

Every community has its own evolved code language for describing landmarks and directions, including up, down, and over. I live near three distinct towns, but when I say I'm going to town I mean to the city of Halifax, otherwise I would name which town. When I lived in one of those towns, I confess that we giggled when new neighbours referred to the main street, one block away, as the village. We thought it sounded so pretentious, because we didn't say it.

That happens anywhere, as the survey respondent said. The clues are fun to identify and easy to share, however, and many of us would be happy to lead a newcomer on an amusing romp through our confusing localisms. A hot or cold adult beverage might be good to go with (some do just say go with). That'd be some good (meaning all good). It'd be right nice to do, right? (The first right rhymes with gate, but the second might be pronounced as 'roite'). There are alot-alot (more than a lot; many) of sayings like those. Back in Chapter 1, when I mentioned that Nova Scotia has a lot of university students, I was tempted to write 'alot-alot' then because that's where you might hear it used, but I hadn't explained it to you yet.

If you're tempted to introduce a new Nova Scotian to your wit along with some home brew, go easy on them. They may be entertained or they may just be feeling the swish.

If you are a newcomer to our shores, wade right in; ask about the phrases you hear that you don't understand. Just don't expect to hear the whole of our *patois* in one sitting. Not all of us think we talk funny, and most of us really don't, most of the time. Our localisms are just that – local – so what you pick up in Margaree may not be what you detect in Pugwash. Some are vestiges of former mother tongues, long forgotten. Others of us just keep to the middle of the linguistic road, and some of us are newcomers, just like you.

If we encourage conversations about language, a veil would be drawn aside, the veil of assumption that everyone knows what we're talking about. Strangers would feel less strange.

From Away
By Catherine Dowdell

I did not
fly as the crow nor
slither as the snake or
slide like the otter

I did not prod
I plopped
down right in
your midst
I look funny to you and
say things you would never say

Jan Fancy Hull

Fitting in and sticking out

Survey responses

CFAs (which I call them in a loving way) are just less fortunate – they didn't have the privilege of growing up here. The only time they cause me angst is when they decide they need to change everything to the way it was wherever they came from...some change is always good, but I often want to ask, "If it is so bad here, then why did you come?"
Thankfully most CFAs are not like this, and they are wonderful positive contributors to our community.
<>
NS is not really interested in embracing CFAs as being part of the old stock Nova Scotians.
<>
My observation has been that so many newcomers to this province see potential and spend their energy enriching the place by starting businesses, creative or otherwise. In my opinion, newcomers bring a whole lot of culture to a province where people I encountered may be a touch close-minded at times.
<>
Neighbours ignore me. My attempt to be a part of the community was not successful. I was on a board for a while, but my attempts to speak to issues were ignored or dismissed. I was handy for a quorum, though. Having ideas different from others, or having experiences in other locations seems to be a detriment in rural NS. You just aren't trusted to have any value to contribute.
This was also an issue in job search for me and my friends.

Anna Shoub has brewed a coffee for me while we talk in her home in Lunenburg (pop. 2,260) about new ideas clashing with old ways.

"Change is part of every community," she says. "Families move out, others move in. Communities are not static, or they die. It can be hard to keep up with how the changes occur. It's not okay to move to a fishing community and then complain about the smell – but locals may also mind the smell and not try to change things. In Lunenburg, there is a divide – and I found it – but you can also look away. You have to stop and look at what's good. There's bureaucracy, the status quo, but there are other things, good things – even with the people you're fighting against."

Anna moved with her husband and young son to Lunenburg about a decade ago, after living in Montreal; Toronto; New York City; Marblehead, Massachusetts; and upstate New York. She says she does recite the whole list when asked, but "Lunenburg is the one that feels like home. I've never been so welcomed in my life. We rented an apartment sight unseen when we first arrived. The landlord was welcoming. Then there was a knock on the door and a woman was there with a plate of scones. She'd heard that I was a milliner, and wanted some things made. I had a four-year-old; that helped. The locals warmed up once they saw we were staying, and that we were a kind of 'heritage family' – a milliner, a woodworker, and a child in school."

Her business, The Hat Junkie, which she operates from her home, ran into some zoning laws. Sorting them out was a contentious and fractious time for Anna, but she is tenacious as well as creative, and the situation was eventually resolved.

Who is a Lunenburger?
2016 blog entry by Peter Zwicker

What makes a Lunenburger? For me this is really quite a simple question and has a relatively straightforward answer:

1. You have chosen to make Lunenburg your home, and/or
2. You were born here.

That makes you a Lunenburger.

In fact, I don't really think you need to live in Lunenburg to make this claim. There is a lot of pride in either being born in Lunenburg, having lived in Lunenburg, or now living in Lunenburg. Even when I lived in New Brunswick and Halifax I always referred to myself as a Lunenburger.

Lunenburg has brand recognition. You can travel to many places on this globe, you mention Lunenburg, and chances are people will know about our great community, or have visited. Lunenburg is a great place to live. I mean, why else live here? People do not typically reside in places they dislike.

To my knowledge, there is no citizenship/residency test you have to take. It doesn't matter where you reside in the parameters of the four square kilometres, how long you have been here, etc.

It's a decision and a frame of mind. Billy Joel sang of a "New York State of Mind." We sing of a Lunenburg state of mind, laid back, breathing the fresh air and living the dream.

Everyone that lives in Lunenburg, or ever has lived in Lunenburg, came from somewhere else, with probably a few exceptions. I will leave that to the historians. Some of us have been here a little longer than others.

Enough is enough with the discussion. Wear that badge proud!

"Resistance to change – that's sheer ignorance," says Pam Mood in Yarmouth. "We are our own worst enemies. We fight everything, until it's done – and then we love it, or most do; some people will never be convinced. It takes strong leadership. You plow ahead because you have a vision. Despite objections. Leadership gets us out of the holes we habitually fall into."

If Pam Mood's comments have you shouting "Yes!" at this page, please vote in the next election – municipal, provincial or federal.

Vote to keep us out of those habitual holes. Vote for quality leadership.

Ever-decreasing voter turnout will jeopardize progress. In the 1960 provincial election, voter turnout was 82%. In the 2017 provincial election, of the 748,630 registered electors in Nova Scotia, only 400,900 cast a ballot — less than 54%. In one riding, just over 40% of electors cast their vote.

The premier, whose party won the 2017 election, said "we need to take a hard look at what we do" to increase turnout. Another party leader stated that "people are not happy with the system." I can find no evidence that anyone took those hard looks or increased our happiness with our electoral system since then. We'll need better leadership on that subject before elections will once again reflect the will of the majority or anything close to it. Increased turnout means more people will be paying attention following the election. That's better for the voters, maybe not for those who get elected.

Unrelated to the zoning issue, Anna Shoub posted a notice on Facebook that she was looking for help in her shop. The person who answered the call was a tailor, a Syrian man recently settled in Mahone Bay, who was hoping to bring his wife's family to Nova Scotia. He soon became busy with his own tailor shop in the area.

> *Survey response*
>
> *My neighbourhood has great interest in the Syrian families who have moved here in the last year. Not so interested in anyone else. The tension seems to be with people who came to the town five to ten years ago and are frustrated with what they see as slow growth and resistance from 'established families.'*

One of Nova Scotia's most fervent seasonal residents is Judith Varney Burch. She owns a sprawling, two hundred year old house with a wide ocean view in Kingsburg. She is a US citizen, "but I'm just renting in Virginia. Kingsburg is home."

She says she would move permanently to Nova Scotia in a heartbeat if she could, but there's the pesky matter of citizenship; US citizens can't stay in Canada for more than six months per year. "I should've applied for citizenship years ago. It seemed like a lot of paperwork and I just didn't get around to it," Judith says with much regret.

When she says "years ago," Judith means half a century. "I first came to Nova Scotia in 1952 as a fourteen-year-old with my parents, from Keewanee, Illinois, where I was Hog Princess. In the seventies, with my husband and three kids, we camped at Kejimkujik. Then we bought a house in Stonehurst. I told my kids, 'If you can't find something good about everyone in this community, there's something wrong with you.' That house had no indoor bathroom, so after five years we looked around, and have subsequently bought four houses in this area."

Judith's kids wouldn't have had far to go to meet the people they were ordered to find good in. Stonehurst is a tiny, rocky cove near Lunenburg, with houses perched close to the salt water on rock outcroppings, a fisher and photographer's dream. I once checked the real estate listings for Stonehurst: there was a converted fisherman's house, with three bedrooms, two baths, kitchen, septic field, living room, family room, games room, foyer, and decks. The price: $420,000 Canadian. Times change.

Judith's life's work arose from those summer visits to our coastal communities. "I first saw Inuit art at a gallery that specialized in it in Lunenburg. I had never heard of it before and I was intrigued. Eventually, I went to Nunavut to meet the people and get a sense of the land where the art was made. Since then, with funding from entities like Canadian embassies, I've travelled around the world to show Inuit art and culture."

She doesn't exaggerate: Judith has presented exhibitions and lectures on Inuit art in China, Asia, Mexico, Mongolia, India, Latvia, Moscow, Siberia, Paris, Buenos Aires, Patagonia, Argentina, and the Smithsonian in Washington DC, and has crossed the Arctic Circle. She has celebrated her eightieth birthday, but has no plans to retire from sharing her love for the culture of these First People.

With all that travel, all those different cultures, did she feel like a stranger anywhere?

"All places felt the same – very welcoming," says Judith. "Except one place, because of one person who just didn't connect well with people."

A lifelong meeter and greeter, Judith Varney Burch is still at it when she is home in Nova Scotia. "I know so many people here; I've been coming here so long. I knew more people [in the US] but they died. I'm busy here trying to meet all the newcomers to this community."

Survey response

I mostly hang out with CFAs, but find the locals very friendly. I try to be very friendly. I try to be inclusive and welcoming to people from other places as I know what it's like to move to a new place. I don't know what it's like to be a visible minority, or non-English-speaking, so I try to welcome newcomers from other places. Recently a friend who is a visible minority who has been here for about six years told me that CFAs are more friendly than locals who already have an established circle of family and friends. I am interested in how to get beyond "hello" with newcomers.

In the hamlet of Petit-Ruisseau, Jay LeBlanc says she has never felt lonely because she felt so connected to the landscape itself. She admits, "It wouldn't be me greeting the newcomers," because she is a self-described recluse, and is uncomfortable sticking out. "But if I'm walking by and they're out, I'll say hi. My neighbours are very helpful to me and I'm here for them."

Jay has a studio in her house where she creates abstract stained glass art. "When the new tourist info centre opened, they put a photo of me and my artwork in it. To me, that meant I was recognized as being 'from here' – perhaps not a big thing, but it was big to me."

In the right context, sticking out can feel good.

From the outside, any group or community or club that a person hopes to join may appear cohesive, unified, a collection of friends. Perceptions can be deceiving. Not all clubs or neighbourhoods are populated with like-minded individuals, not all the time anyway, or about all topics. It's difficult enough to fit in if the group has divisions, even more so if those divisions are not readily discernible.

Born and raised in her community of Middle New Cornwall, Kathy Rafuse has lived among friends and relations all her life. She doesn't see herself ever going away from home for long. "I'd probably break down in three weeks and come home," she admits. While her situation may seem ideal to those who seek to put down deep roots like hers, it has its challenges that need to be managed. Kathy says when fractious incidents arise it's best to just let go of them.

"Being involved [in a community] for a lifetime, you're bound to rub somebody the wrong way, or vice versa. If you can't get over it, you're doomed, as nobody's going anywhere."

Survey responses

For the most part all neighbours were friendly and very helpful. As in most communities there is always that one dictator neighbour of sorts.

<>

I was born in NS and have lived in various parts of it for most of my life. I was a newcomer in one small community...and had the experience of being accosted on my property by neighbours who considered me to be a rank newcomer, doing things differently from their ways, and was told if I didn't like how things were done here, I should go back where I came from. I was totally flabbergasted, never having been spoken to in such a way anywhere in my home province, or anywhere else. However, I came to realize that those neighbours were themselves very odd, so I got over the event...
most folks were and are kind and pleasant.

Go back where you came from? For shame. That does nothing to resolve any differences. Sure, disagreements will arise between neighbours, maybe about a barking dog (it shouldn't be your barking dog) or other perceived faults.

People who once were newcomers themselves may be less likely to tell more recent newcomers to go back; that weapon could backfire on them. Newcomers understand the challenges of fitting in, and they may make friends with each other more easily than with the locals. As new neighbours settle in, their opinions, preferences and rights must be counted just as much as anyone else's.

"We have Syrian refugees here in Yarmouth now," Pam Mood says. "We honour their pain, and then we look for the potential they bring to the community. This is home now for them. We try to make their life normal, and that means working and meeting their community."

Pam herself is the granddaughter of immigrants, and that informs her approach to refugees. Her grandparents were focused on assimilating, forging a new home here for themselves and their family – as newcomers do today. Pam is now exploring her Lebanese heritage, picking up the cultural threads her grandparents had dropped while they were busy surviving and assimilating.

Telling someone to go back is as bigoted as telling Vanessa Fells that the neighbours "don't want you here". This may come as cold comfort to newcomers, but my survey responses and interviews show that even long-time Nova Scotians aren't always welcoming to each other, let alone to new neighbours who came from foreign lands. Kathy Rafuse's advice to "get over it", as the survey respondent apparently did, is wise, but hard to follow. Even more reason to greet new neighbours with a token gift of welcome.

Survey response

Are we glad we live here? Yes, we love the life away from the hustle and bustle of city life, and the friendliness of the people. Genuine people. Not concerned with keeping up to the Joneses. When I first came back, much of my crystal was broken and I no longer had a matching set. I apologized, and the response was that if you have a glass and something to put in it, then alleluia, aren't we fortunate.
That became my mantra and affects much of my life. Love it.

Cookies are good-neighbour currency. "I'm a neighbourhood busy-body," says Kacy Petersen DeLong, who lives near the hamlet of Barss Corner, "so I'm generally one of the first people at the door of a new neighbour. If I'm less busy, I might take cookies; otherwise I'll just show up. Sometimes they're surprised. I'm surprised that people seem surprised to meet their neighbours. We just talk on the doorstep for ten minutes."

Kacy moved from Halifax to her rural community, but when I ask if she was ever a newcomer, she answers, "No. I say that because I didn't feel like a newcomer. I moved here on purpose, planned to move here, married here. I had the status of a newcomer but not the mentality of one. It's not like I have to row my dory two days to get to the next bay over; I can drive to Halifax in an hour. Two years ago, I was still relatively unknown in this community. One year ago, I started my business; then I was known and recognized."

Kacy joined the committee for a refugee family reunification project in nearby Mahone Bay. The tailor from Damascus who had responded to Anna Shoub's job posting, with his wife and little boy, hoped to bring their extended family to Nova Scotia. I attended one of the project's public meetings. After the presentation, someone brought around a plate of "Syrian cookies." The one I ate tasted very good. A lot like Canadian cookies.

Kacy Petersen DeLong also volunteered, with an organization in Halifax which repairs bicycles to give to newcomers. "I thought it was important to support newcomers, so I drove to Halifax every Friday to learn how to repair bikes, and to teach newcomers how to navigate the streets. Think of it: if you're new to the city, how do you get around? How do you take the bus?"

I'm wondering how many decades have passed since I last took the bus in Halifax. I know where things are, but not what bus would get me there.

"The goal is to put this service more in the hands of the new Canadians themselves. Then they can share what they've found with other newcomers, and explain the differences and challenges their way."

Kacy always refers to refugees as "new Canadians" or "our new friends." I ask her about her careful language. "Once they're here, they are Canadians, like us," she replies. "I'm a friendly person, but there's a lot I didn't know, so I took the ISANS (Immigrant Services Association of Nova Scotia) Inter-Cultural Competencies course in preparation for working on the bikes. As you get involved, you realize there isn't a gap to bridge."

Survey response

Home is a community, and I don't think communities can be any stronger than in rural Nova Scotia.

"I've been welcoming newcomers since I was five years old," says Kathy Rafuse. "There was a little school here, but it closed in 1964, so I took the bus to school in Blockhouse. One time, a new girl came and I was asked to look out for her when she got on the bus. We're still friends."

All sorts of friendly greeting was going on in Kathy's neighbourhood, especially in the summers. "There's a subdivision behind here [on a lake]. They weren't – and aren't – Come From Aways, they're Cabin People. There were about thirty cottages, though many of the owners have permanent homes here now. Cabin People would meet the locals at the tiny store, run by an aunt. Many Cabin People married local people. They live here now and their grandchildren are here."

That's a great way to build a community, as The Farmer's Daughter Market is doing in Cape Breton. The store Kathy refers to has been closed up for a long time, but the tiny building still stands by the road. It's smaller than any of the outbuildings I saw around the Whycocomagh market, but it was large enough to serve as a community catalyst.

Cookies or casseroles are simply tokens of welcome to "our new friends." Sure, fewer people bake anything these days, but a loaf of bread from the local bakery wouldn't go awry, or a bundle of kindling wrapped in ribbon, or something from the garden, or a jar of jam from the local market.

> *Survey response*
>
> *We moved from Banff. People [here] were very welcoming,*
> *especially those that have travelled or are*
> *from elsewhere themselves.*
> *Neighbours came by with home-made jam and now we are*
> *best friends.*

"Maybe shovelling snow" would be a good way to meet and greet neighbours, suggests Jennifer Watts in Halifax. "Or maybe taking muffins to those newly moved in. There are a variety of ways of being welcoming. Community gardens are good for involving newcomers and the resident community; growing food is a great way to connect. Volunteering, too. One gets lost so much in the business/busyness of living, and things change, your children grow, work changes. If you have kids or dogs, those are the automatic connectors with your neighbours and neighbourhood."

"In Canada, we strongly convey the expectation that newcomers will become new Canadians," Jennifer says, "hence all the assistance offered by agencies like Immigrant Services Association of Nova Scotia." Jennifer is CEO of ISANS, which offers the course that Kacy Petersen DeLong enrolled in to prepare herself to work with newcomers.

I asked Jennifer if there is any pushback from local communities against ISANS' work. "Not really. There is an awareness of needing to support immigrants. There is a sense of compassion and welcoming for them."

It may not be indecision about whether the new neighbours are wheat-intolerant or vegan that holds us back. The physical act of knocking on a stranger's door may be daunting. Welcome Wagon created a business doing what people wanted done but didn't want to do themselves.

Welcome Wagon's website describes their operation as "a Canadian national service that provides visits and organizes events in over 500 communities across the country. Partnering with local businesses from coast to coast, we assist families with lifestyle changes, such as moving to a new neighbourhood, getting married or having a baby. From in-home visits to bridal shows and family events, we help thousands of Canadians every month."

Knocking on doors, once a busy commercial activity, especially appreciated in rural areas where seeing new faces and new products was an almost-unreachable dream, has fallen out of favour in the twenty-first century. Some newcomers may also be reluctant to open their door to strangers in their new neighbourhood. That's no problem, Welcome Wagon says; they'll just email coupons from local businesses to the newcomers if they sign up for them. Coupons are something, but they're not a handshake.

Survey response

> *[This town] is very accepting of CFAs as there are*
> *a great many of us here.*

Tina Hennigar didn't wait for anyone to welcome her into her new hometown. She grew up on her family's small pig farm in Canning in the Annapolis Valley, "back when small farming wasn't cool," she says. "When I was in Grade Two we moved to Bridgewater (pop. 8,532) where I lived until I was nineteen." She didn't have much desire or ability to see new horizons until she finished school. Then she drove herself to nearby Mahone Bay (pop. 1,036) for the first time.

"Culture shock! I had never been there! I drove through the town for the first time, went to the market, was impressed by the bag of carrots on a pulley that keeps the screen door closed, was moved by the three churches, stopped in at the pub – it all felt like home. I got talking to the bartender – and got hired on."

It happened pretty much that quickly and easily for gregarious Tina. "If you want to fit into a community, get a job at the local pub," she advises. "I met the mayor there, and then his wife, who invited me to join things. I met this guy who came in often, I learned his name – and we've been married for over twenty years now, with two kids."

Now Tina considers herself an unofficial greeter for the town as well as officially for the enterprise called NOW Lunenburg County. "I'm always thanking new people for moving here. We are very welcoming, I think." Well, she is, for one.

What makes her so keen? "When my family moved to Bridgewater, the community really welcomed and supported us. So I just felt that any community would be lucky to have me! How do you make people feel welcome? You include them in things as people did for my family back then, and for me when I moved to Mahone Bay."

Survey response

No, I wouldn't ever move away. Yes, there is crap to put up with,
but meet the right people and life here is amazing.
The place is beautiful.

Let's ask Jessie Hatt about fitting in. She and her husband Steven live in Vogler's Cove (pop. 200), a sweet little coastal village with a park, a community centre, and a wharf where their lobster boat, *The Gambler,* is tied up when I visit. It is lobster season, but Steven is waiting until the strong winds pushing up six-meter waves outside the cove subside. Jessie is Status Mi'kmaq; her husband is not Indigenous.

"When we first came here to Vogler's Cove," Jessie tells me, "I went to fisheries school to get my lobster license, and graduated – the very first Mi'kmaq woman to get a commercial lobster license! But I couldn't be proud and loud here. Natives didn't need a license to fish, you see, and people just assumed our boat was paid for by the Band. It wasn't."

She wasn't interested in settling for the 'moderate livelihood' that Indigenous people are permitted by Treaty to take from fishing. She was interested in earning a good living in the industry.

"Then, even though Steven's family are from here and are non-native, our son was mocked at school, kids making 'war-whoops' at him, calling him names the kids would have learned at home, like 'wagon-burner.' So we had to confront racism at school and on the school bus."

I'm sitting with Jessie at her kitchen table, while Steven listens in from their living room, but I have the sensation I'm standing on the deck of their boat at sea when she speaks: it's invigorating and a little disorienting. I hold on tight: she has strongly-held opinions, and delivers them rapid-fire, but without malice.

"I love this community," she says. "And my neighbours."

Jessie was born in Mi'kma'qi (traditional Mi'kmaq territory), though not in Nova Scotia. "My family had been in Bear River, but my grandfather was determined that his two youngest children, one of whom was my mother, would not go to those residential schools as his other children had, so they moved to Massachusetts and Maine. I have dual US and Canadian citizenship."

I ask if there are newcomers in Vogler's Cove. "There are," she says. "Many are from the Worcester area. Massachusetts and Lunenburg County accents are similar, so we can get pretty funny with each other. I like the diversity here. Just like my own family: I and my siblings don't have the same father, just the same mother. My father was Irish."

Jessie says when her family lived on a reservation in Cambridge in the Annapolis Valley, "they would have to get permission to leave the reservation so they could take the train to Halifax to sell baskets in the market. There would be punishment if they were late returning. It was our land, reserved for us, but we couldn't leave it without permission from the 'Indian Man' – who was not Indian."

Jessie takes issue with much more than white people acting as gate-keepers. "I'm no fan of the Band Councils or the reservation system. My grandfather worked at anything, anywhere, as a guide in Kejimkujik, picking blueberries, construction, anything. Living on the reservation, I grew up thinking that having no regular job was 'the Indian way.' We [she and Steven] left the reservation because we didn't want our son to grow up there. We have to play catch-up, learning our culture and language, and this is not offered on the reservation. My mother didn't speak a word of our language. Grandmother did, but we kids weren't allowed to speak Mi'kmaq."

She continues, "My mother was 'go along to get along.' Not me. She was born on the res. She hated that system. She wanted the 'white woman house.' My grandmother was a staunch Catholic, even after everything they did. So much of our culture has been lost. You see photographs of our elders wearing skins with knitted long underwear underneath – really? What were the practices before the settlers? Nobody knows. They were not written down, and the few petroglyphs that have been found don't show any people or describe what they did."

I ask her about the practice at some events to announce that they are held on un-ceded Mi'kmaq territory, as described in Chapter 1. "That's beside the point. It's not answering a question," she states. "The new accords that some are trying to negotiate will bypass our Treaties. Our Treaties were ratified, and should be observed."

Driving home afterward, I wonder if Jessie's valley relatives, taking their baskets eastward by train to the market in Halifax, ever met anybody from Beverly Hugli's eastern shore community, taking their clams westward by train to the same market.

Survey response

If you are a visible minority, the level of both overt and covert racism drives people away, [but] if they do stay, you hear lots of racist comments about stealing jobs etc.
Gets tiring having to do racism 101 for people!

As an adult in Nova Scotia, Vanessa Fells still experiences the sting of racism. "It's a big problem, above and beyond anything else: comments, being followed in stores, you know the looks. It's a big problem, but it's so subtle."

Sometimes it's not subtle. While we were sitting in the main exhibit space at the Black Loyalist Heritage Centre in Birchtown (pop. 200), where she was Public Outreach and Community Coordinator, Vanessa shared a recent racist encounter. "Just two weeks ago, when I was walking in a shopping mall, a hairdresser, who had a client in the chair, yelled out the door at me as I walked by: 'Hey! You need to get a new hairstyle!'"

Vanessa is hard to ignore: she's tall, has great posture, and she wears her hair big. To that so-called stylist, an Afro may be a style that white kids wore in the previous century to show they were hip. To people of African descent, with African hair, the comment is – well, I ask Vanessa how she felt. "It's about him, not me," she generously replies.

As well as generous, Vanessa Fells is educated. She received a Bachelor's degree in sociology and legal studies at Acadia University in Wolfville, studied criminology and legal subjects at Saint Mary's University in Halifax and in Ottawa, and earned a Master's in Education from Mount Saint Vincent University in Halifax. Like Jessie Hatt, she made sure she was qualified to have the future she wanted for herself.

At the Black Loyalist Centre, the exhibits are very moving. 'No bread. No land. Free, but not equal' proclaims one banner. I ask Vanessa if she thinks things are changing for the better for the Black community in Nova Scotia.

"I think so," she says. "Look at what's happened in the last twenty years: this Centre, Africville, others. Sure, there are protests. I have absolutely no problem with protests. But just holding a sign and screaming doesn't do it. You need education and political change, too. The UN declared 2015 to 2024 as the International Decade for People of African Descent: Recognition, Justice and Development. Protests and political action are both needed."

Would she leave Nova Scotia? "Nova Scotia is home," she says. "It's important to me to teach the next generation, especially African Nova Scotians, to learn who they are, to get a sense of pride. But yes, I would move away – probably – for work, maybe international work."

That's not just day-dreaming. She currently works in Cherry Brook as Program Coordinator for the African Nova Scotia Decade for People of African Descent Coalition.

"But I would always come back, because it's home, though with technology, family are just a screen away. But there's the ocean, too..."

Change doesn't happen by itself: it is voted for, and it takes leadership from strong people like Jessie Hatt and Vanessa Fells. Add at least two more chairs to that virtual café table.

'Values Test' doesn't stand the test of Canadian history
By Peter Stoffer in the Chronicle Herald, 2016

On September 26, 2016, I celebrated the 60th anniversary of my family's arrival in Canada. My mom and dad and six kids (aged 15 years to 9 months) left Rotterdam and came to Pier 21 in Halifax in search of a better life.

This got me thinking about my former Conservative parliamentary colleagues Kelly Leitch and Tony Clement – and about their recent comments stating that new immigrants should be screened to adhere to "Canadian values."

Jan Fancy Hull

> But let's look back at Canada in 1956 – to what would be considered "Canadian values" at that time.
>
> It was OK to beat the Indian out of the indigenous child, to rip those children out of their homes, to have many of them suffer from sexual and physical abuse at the hands of so-called religious and government institutions.
>
> It was acceptable to openly discriminate against our African brothers and sisters.
>
> It was OK to jail gay or lesbian people and to fire them from their place of employment.
>
> It was commonplace to sexually harass women in the workplace.
>
> It was standard practice to openly pollute our air, soil and water – to have one drink for the road and to smoke openly in public places.
>
> My thanks to the government of the day for not asking my parents, on behalf of my family, to accept our so-called Canadian standards at the time.
>
> You see, Kelly and Tony, Canadian values have changed in 60 years.
>
> And even though we're nowhere near where we should be as an equal society, we are moving forward.
>
> But we trust the day will come when Canada – and the world, for that matter – reaches respect, equality, and dignity for all persons.
>
> As J.S. Woodworth once said, "What we desire for ourselves, we wish for all."
>
> Thank you, Canada.

Kejimkujik National Park has been a treasured place for millennia. Jessie Hatt's grandfather guided tourists who came there to hunt and fish. Judith Varney Burch's family camped there in the 1970s. Greg Selig began camping there one year after it opened in 1968.

"There were some hard feelings in the community about the park," Greg says, "because the Federal government expropriated land for it, removing old lodges and sites where First Nations guides had earned their livelihood. Now, there is some attempt at reconciliation."

Greg Selig and his partner, Janis Power, are assembling sandwiches for our lunch at their picnic table in the park, which most campers call Keji, while water for their morning coffee comes to a boil on the propane camp stove. It is already noon, but they had visitors until late the night before, and they're holidaying in a campground, so who cares what time it is? The late July air is cool in the shade of the heavily-treed campsite. No problem: it keeps the black flies down.

Greg and Janis are Campground Hosts at Keji. The National Parks website describes the job: *Hosts provide a warm, welcoming atmosphere at our campgrounds. They greet visitors upon arrival, visit campers' sites, and also invite people into their 'host site' to share information.*

It's a good gig: hosts get to stay free in the campground, but in return they must be on site during their time. Hosts have to deal with unruly campers or excessive noise, but that happens rarely. I expect cheerful Greg and soft-spoken Janis, assisted by their little dog, handle most people very well.

We're talking about community, and how one is welcomed into one. It's complicated. "We've lost a sense of community over the years," Greg says, "one in which people knew each other. Now we have a collective community of individuals."

Greg and Janis make their home in New Germany (pop. 447). It's an active community, thanks in good measure to Greg's efforts, among others. "We don't have many church suppers or Sunday School picnics [like before]. Church parking lots on Sunday mornings have few cars. Churches are becoming irrelevant; old people still go, but not young people, and church attitudes are sometimes at odds with changing values."

It takes a lot of energy to organize and sustain a community event, even when it's enjoyed and appreciated. "We held Meet & Greets in New Germany, open to the whole community, especially people who had businesses," Greg says. "The first and second ones went well, but I was the only one doing the inviting for the third. I organize a Health Expo now, so I have no time to do another Meet & Greet."

Greg is a persistent greeter. I ask him when was the last time he greeted a newcomer, or at least someone he didn't recognize. "Yesterday, in line at the grocery store," he says. "I just ask people where they're from."

Months later, on a bitterly cold December day, I stood in line to pick up my lobster order from fishers who deliver to New Germany. There's Greg strolling along, saying hello to everyone, though most of us were so bundled in scarves I'm not sure how he knew who was who.

Back in July's cool (but not freezing) Keji campsite, I mention the survey respondent who lamented about "no cake, no casserole, and no welcome visit."

"It happens," Greg says. "People of different colour, language, or sexual orientation will have that experience sometimes." Greg doesn't appear inclined to hold a whole community responsible for the actions of one person's neighbours, though he would do things differently himself.

There's a sign posted at the entrance to their Keji campsite:

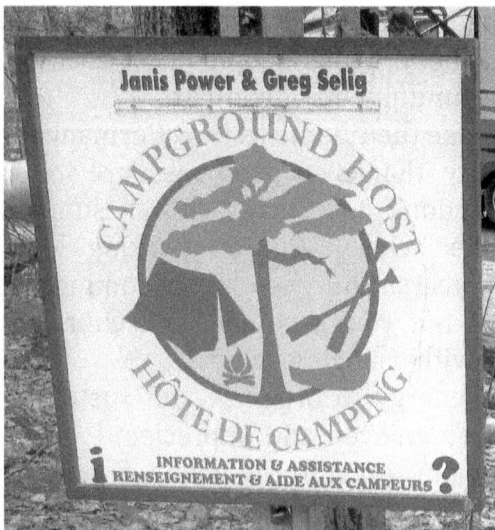

It occurs to me how nice it would be if there were hosts in all our communities, with a little sign like that at the end of someone's driveway to welcome newcomers and help them fit in. Municipalities or Chambers of Commerce could easily coordinate that.

As I back my car out of their campsite, Greg calls out, "Have I invited you yet to the community pot-luck picnic in New Germany?"

The Biggest of the Little Towns
by Steve Skafte on social media, 2016

Winter has come to my hometown. She is aching in her shivering, I feel it in my tips. Nose, fingers, lips, blown in on a dusting of snow. I've been a son of Bridgetown since being born, and I still walk Queen Street with the same bright, strange sense of wonder. There's an aching I can't express, a lonely, friendly beauty that comes with the coming of darkness, and Christmas.

Who are you in your small town, sheltering? Who keeps warm within the walls of this village of a thousand souls? Do they know you, do they recognize your face and say your name when you pass by? This is a place of beautiful buildings, some aging more gracefully than others. They watch me in the evening, long after the shop lights flicker out and everyone else rushes inside to warm their frozen feet by the fire.

I could cry right now, it wouldn't take much. Twenty-nine years I've lived in this biggest of the little towns, and it all wells up like rushing water freshly frozen over. I swear that I could crack, and no one could blame me for it. So I just say, "Welcome home," even if you've never been here before. If you want to be a Nova Scotian, welcome home.

Jan Fancy Hull

4 – Routes vs Roots

Survey responses

Home is the location I presently live in...I don't call my birth-place home...

<>

Home is where my Mum is. Nova Scotia is most certainly home. I hope to return to live with my husband (British Columbian) this year! There are a lot of logistics, jobs is a big one. Weather is a big one.

<>

I would love to move back to NS but I have built a life in Ontario with a husband and children, as well as a job. I also have family living here now. So I don't think I ever will move back.

<>

Although I live in The Netherlands, over the years I still thought of Halifax as my home. My family has dwindled away through deaths and it's getting more difficult to keep calling it home, although it will always be that in my heart. For some reasons, when I first came here, I always thought I could go home, that there would always be a place for me, but now, things have changed so much and it's not so easy anymore.

<>

I left in 1983. Sorry. Headed west to make money. I have lived in northern BC since then. Nova Scotia will always be my home.

Coming back

Many Nova Scotians have moved away in pursuit of love or money, and one hopes they found both. Even when life has worked out fine for them, some feel guilty for abandoning the province, evidenced by that "Sorry" in the survey response.

I believe I speak on behalf of many Nova Scotians when I say, "Don't be sorry. If you want or need to go, go with our blessings. We'll miss you, but we'll be fine." I know Pam Mood would agree; she said it's natural for young people to go away. We don't want to guilt them into returning, but we can try to attract them.

The seventies revue *The Rise and Follies of Cape Breton Island* included the song, "Go Off on Your Way, Now" by Ronnie Maceachern, with this poignant chorus:

> Go off on your way, now, and may you find better things.
> Don't wait around 'til you have no fare to leave.
> All the best if you're stayin', and all the best if you should choose to leave.
> Here's to kindness on your journey.
> Here's to joy in your new home.

Survey responses

We returned home 27 years ago. We're still considered newcomers and we get along with everyone.

<>

I returned to Nova Scotia after a 30-year absence, but to a new town. The neighbours were initially friendly but not very curious and we've been unable to establish new friendships and have felt quite shut out at a number of community activities.

If you do want to return home, well, that's complicated, too. Home may not be here now.

Lloyd and Maude Bailey are as homeless as a well-to-do couple can be. "Home is where the motor home is parked," Lloyd says. "We've lived all over the world for fifty years, so although Cape Breton County was home, there's not much appeal there now. Nothing to do. In Kuwait, there are health clubs, restaurants – but it's all city, no country. Tim Horton's is there, but it's not the same as in Canada. Cape Breton, by contrast, is all rural, all Tim Horton's. But we always say we're from Cape Breton."

Lloyd is retired from the Canadian Air Force; Maude is a teacher. Both now teach at international private schools in Kuwait City. So, where's home for them? They're silent for a moment. "We don't know," is their joint answer. "Kuwait City? Motor home? Cape Breton for a visit? It doesn't matter."

Teaching abroad will come to an end sometime. Do they have plans? "Our goal was to live in Ontario, near our family, but our family may move at any time to follow their own careers. Our two daughters are both in Ontario, not connected to Nova Scotia as they were born away."

Lloyd joined the Air Force in 1963, and the couple moved every three to five years. "We always came home to Cape Breton between postings. Family was there. When our parents passed away, it didn't hold the same meaning, though we did have a beautiful view of the Bras d'Or. We'll likely end up near our daughters. Maybe. Full circle."

They did try coming home again. "We were 'returners.' We renovated a home in Cape Breton and moved there in 2010. We semi-connected with one couple, but we could never really connect. We're not the joining type. The residents have changed since we lived there. So we decided to sell. Our family members who oversaw the renovations for us felt betrayed when we sold."

I didn't fly to Kuwait City to interview the Baileys, but I was in Florida when they were there for a Christmas visit with family and friends. They took time out from helping to prepare a community Christmas dinner in a mobile home park where they had owned units, and where Lloyd had served as the residents' association president. There is much friendly banter with other volunteers in the clubhouse as we talk. They seem very much at home, perhaps because most other folk there are snowbirds, meaning also from somewhere else.

Lloyd wouldn't be one to say 'sorry' for leaving home. As a young man in North Sydney, he had a job working for a meat cutter. "When I joined the Air Force as a private, my boss said I shouldn't leave. He said he would send me to meat-cutting school, help me get my certificate. Whenever I returned to North Sydney, the same man was there in the meat department. Then, on one visit, I found the store had closed."

Sandee MacLean in Whycocomagh talked about local businesses mentoring workers to learn a trade so they can stay in the community and earn a good living. Those enterprises must remain viable to keep their workers employed for a lifetime, not easy in small communities with shrinking populations. Lloyd chose a different path, and retired with the rank of Major, with a good pension and ongoing employment opportunities, just not at home.

Survey responses

Most that leave Nova Scotia eventually return.

<>

I believe that no matter who you are, if you are from Nova Scotia you will most likely come home, if not to live, at least to visit again.

While I was visiting friends in Alabama, the southern US state where Kris Srivatsa did his medical residency, I interviewed Liz Smith (not her real name), who teaches and conducts research at a university there. Born and raised in Halifax, Liz left home at eighteen to attend university in New Brunswick, then Ontario, then British Columbia, over the next decade.

"I knew I wasn't going to stay in those places," she says. "I knew they were temporary. Where I would go next became more uncertain as I progressed in my education." Her specialty isn't taught everywhere, and where research grants are available is a significant factor in where she may choose to live.

Liz lives with her husband Robert and their busy toddler in a new house in a new subdivision where many other academic families live. "We've been here in Alabama for five years and it really feels like home," Robert says. "Not like BC, where I'm from.

We own a house, we have our baby, and we've met other people who have children and similar interests. We like it here. People have pride in this community. They're friendly and happy. I think friendliness and happiness correlate."

"People are people," Liz says. "Alabama may be more like Nova Scotia than anywhere else I've lived."

Perhaps not politically, but I did have that same impression of the topography when driving around the state, enjoying the rolling hills and pine trees. A recent tornado touch-down had chewed up some of those trees, though, a rarity in Nova Scotia.

I ask if this family would consider moving/returning to Nova Scotia at some point. "Maybe," Liz replies, "if I had a job opportunity. We are Canadians, from a different culture – but the weather here is nicer than Nova Scotia, and it's very affordable here. We aren't opposed to returning home. I recently realized that our baby is 'from here;' this is our baby's home. There are a lot of places where we would be happy. I miss the ocean, but the Gulf of Mexico is only a four-hour drive away. Robert misses the mountains. The terrain here is hilly, though not even the Allegheny Mountains are like the Rockies."

Robert adds, "You can make a decision to like it anywhere. We both prefer not to be in a big city. Most of our friends don't have family here either, so we are the community and support for each other. Some people don't like where they are because they want to be somewhere else, and are living for the moment when that opportunity arrives – if it ever does. So they don't blend in."

Robert's comments seem sensible enough: be happy, decide to like where you are, and it will become your home.

I am reminded of the fable about a traveller who questioned an old man about the people in the nearby town. "What were they like where you came from?" the elder asked. "Not nice at all," the traveller said. "Well, keep on your way," the old man replied. "They're the same here."

The next voyager made the same inquiry, and said the people he'd left behind were friendly as all get out (as we say here, meaning very friendly). "Well then," the old fellow said, "you'll find the same kind of folk here. Do stay."

Looking back

Survey response

"Home" seems to depend on where I am, or where I'm not. It is the other place. My stuff is in Toronto (mostly). My heart is in NS. When people ask me when I'm going home, it is the other place they mean.

Deanne Fitzpatrick was born and raised in Newfoundland, a place she loves, and has lived for some thirty years in Amherst, a place she also loves. "You're culturally of that place where you grew up," Deanne says. "Home is my house in Amherst and the land, where I raised my kids. There are two kinds of home. I am rooted here, but I have roots elsewhere, and there are strong cultural traditions in Newfoundland."

One day in 2015, Deanne began to explore her thoughts and feelings about Newfoundland, about home and belonging and fitting in. An artist in the medium of hooked rugs, Deanne produced an exhibition of twenty-two colourful rugs as a result of those musings. In 2016 The Art Gallery of Nova Scotia purchased her show, called *The Very Mention of Home*, for its permanent collection.

"I love them," Deanne says of her works. "They did the job. People will think of home when they see them."

One of her images is of a row of colourful houses with this caption: 'Will you ever heave a sigh or a wish for me?' This is a line from *The Nova Scotia Song*, collected in the 1930s by folklorist Dr. Helen Creighton. You may recognize the song – especially if you frequent any bar in the world where Nova Scotians gather to buy each other beer.

Farewell to Nova Scotia, the seabound coast.
May your mountains dark and dreary be.
When I am far away, on the briny ocean tossed,
Will you ever heave a sigh or a wish for me?

I ask Deanne why she hooked those words into the piece. "I was missing home a bit," she says, "and wondering...you miss home, but the landscape never misses you. I felt kind of sad that we're just passing through."

We're talking on the phone, but her wistfulness is clearly audible across the wires.

Survey responses

Nova Scotia has always been my home – I just didn't know it until I moved here more than 40 years ago. I instantly fell in love and felt at home here in NS.

<>

To paraphrase Jim Croce: Perth, Australia is home but it's not mine. Truro's mine but it's not home.

Another artist in fabric, Valerie Hearder, stitched her longings for home into art quilts, also exploring the land and her relationship to it. Valerie grew up in South Africa, that warm, bright country that Dal law student Veryan Haysom immigrated from years ago (they are husband and wife).

"I thought I was an emotional weakling because I was missing South Africa," Valerie confesses. "I tried very hard to be Canadian. I wept when leaving South Africa after visits. I grieved."

Several years after establishing their home in Mahone Bay, Valerie and Veryan moved "temporarily" to Newfoundland for Veryan's work. "That went on for seven years, and I became depressed, missing Mahone Bay," Valerie recalls. A friend even scolded her for being so whiny about it.

Between 1954 and 1975, the government of Newfoundland and Labrador resettled 30,000 residents from 300 remote coastal communities to towns where they could have access to schools, government services, and roads. It was very controversial, but that's the story of that beautiful province. While there, Valerie visited some of these abandoned outports, and was moved.

"I was beginning to wonder about what we leave behind when we leave," she says. "It seemed to me that the former residents' spirits were still there, the women in their kitchens keeping the kettle boiling, the men at their wharves. I wondered about what of me I had left behind in South Africa."

Through this time in Newfoundland, Valerie was making and exhibiting her quilts, many featuring landscapes in the vibrant and saturated colours of Africa. Deciding to quilt a scene in Canadian tones, she chose autumn as her subject. She proudly showed it to a friend, who exclaimed, "Oh, it's beautiful, so African!"

Valerie was devastated. How could her experienced artist's eyes betray her so? Fog would come and envelop the Avalon Peninsula for three weeks straight, and when it went away it didn't reveal anything like the South African palette.

Eventually, she was able to see the beauty in the muted North Atlantic light, and she worked with a new appreciation of what was around her. Valerie created a solo exhibition of her quilt art called *Autobiography of Place* with the theme of home, displacement, and belonging. Once she could see it, she loved it.

Or was it the other way around? "It's a universal human story, I think," Valerie says, as we share fruitcake and a pot of roibos tea in her studio. "I began putting my story into the landscape of Newfoundland, even though I was foreign to that landscape. We do bring our original landscape where we grew up, no matter what landscape we live in. I grew to love the different colour palette there."

Eventually, Valerie and Veryan did leave Newfoundland and return to Nova Scotia. "And now I grieve for Newfoundland! But our children and grandchildren live here now, so here is home."

I ask her if she still weeps when leaving South Africa. "No. I made a decision that I didn't have to belong to any one place. I didn't have to choose. I could be a citizen of the world." Valerie found a way to be of two minds about home – or maybe three. She also led cultural tours from Canada to South Africa for six years so she could share the beauty of her homeland with an appreciative group of travellers from her adopted land.

South Africa's struggles with its white settlers are well-known. "Our families have been South African for five generations," Valerie tells me. "When someone said that we should 'go back where we came from,' I wondered where that would be. I have no idea what part of Scotland my people came from, or if it even was Scotland."

Survey response

All who leave try hard to come back. Most leave only for work.

Lydia Adams hopes to return to her Glace Bay homeland someday for longer than a visit. "Well, yes – in a heartbeat. But right now, my work is based here in Ontario. Cape Breton offers space, and also community values – a sense of humour, kindness – to surround myself with. Yes, kindness, which can be greatly missing in our society; it's an important aspect and needs to be emphasized more."

That magnetic sense of belonging can be a torment. We may feel the pull – but to where? Phyllis Price says she feels a sense of belonging in every place she lived, before and including Broad Cove. "It's interesting to think what triggers that," she says. She has made a diagram of her thoughts and adds to it during our conversation. "Being outside, being part of the landscape helps. Maybe there's something in the air…"

We Nova Scotians do love our ocean and our hills. We don't drink or eat them, but many of us do take nourishment from them. Deanne Fitzpatrick in Amherst is saddened to think that rocks and trees are not sentient things that can heave a sigh or a wish for her.

Regardless, we should not discredit the strong pull that we feel toward some places. Jay LeBlanc feels it on her land in Petit-Ruisseau, sensing the land knows her.

I, too, know that feeling. When I arrived at my own lakeside property one sizzling August day, the very air seemed to shimmer with energy. I am always happy to see the place, but that day, I felt like the place was happy to see me.

Deanne Fitzpatrick and Valerie Hearder are both artists who 'paint' with fabric, though in dissimilar styles. Independently of each other, both have depicted 'home' as iconic peaked-roof houses – simple shelters – but telling very different stories. At first, I thought I'd have to choose one for this book, but that was impossible. So I present them both (colour versions are on the back cover). The feelings they portray are deliciously diverse.

'Between Two Places' - hooked rug by Deanne Fitzpatrick

'Safe as Houses' - quilt art by Valerie Hearder

Two minds

British author Jeanette Winterson has written about the concept that every time you make an important choice, the part of you that you left behind continues the other life you could have led. It's not such a crazy notion if you consider that we commonly use the terms 'whole-heartedly' and 'half-heartedly.' We often say we are 'of two minds,' which is usually meant to indicate indecision, but perhaps the phrase could be taken at face value: two rival ideas, residing in one head: nowhere and now here.

You may know the ancient fable about a woman who was killed because she was of two minds about leaving her home. Her story is found in the Jewish, Christian and Muslim traditions. She is perhaps best known as Lot's Wife.

Here is my loose retelling of her story, which is in Genesis, chapter 19 of the Bible, among other texts: God tells Mr Lot to pack up his wife and family and abandon their home tonight. God is going to fire-bomb the town because everyone in town, other than the Lots, is too sinful to let live any longer. The Lots hastily gather a few possessions and flee, as people do to this day, from fires, from floods, from tyrants and bombs. God orders the Lots not to look back. That's harsh.

The Lots were shepherds, so one imagines flocks of sheep grazing on green hills around their town, a beautiful scene. Overcome with longing to see her beloved landscape for the last time before it is destroyed, Mrs Lot takes one look back – and is turned into a pillar of salt. Ouch!

Naturally-occurring, free-standing, salt rock formations near the Dead Sea are now known as Lot's Wife.

Looking back as we leave home is a natural impulse, one that many modern-day women and men cannot resist. Luckily, the punishment in these latter days is not to be turned into a rock formation. It's spiritual unrest, a consequence not to be taken lightly.

> *Survey response*
>
> *Lots of neighbours, love getting together with them. One peeve:*
> *They come because they like it here –*
> *so don't change it to make it where they came from!*

We may develop an undertone of resentment of people who come to our communities and then tell us how nice their former home was, how smart everyone there was, all the great things they had and did. It makes us uncomfortable, unless the former home is 'back home' here in Nova Scotia. When people come here from troubled countries, we don't want them marching in our cold, gray streets to protest about the regimes they left behind. We're suspicious of what foreign ways they might bring with them to the best country in the world, though multiculturalism is a significant part of what makes us best.

In these pages, we've met a number of Nova Scotians whose ancestors did not come from Scotland on the ship *Hector* – and we're richer for all of them having been here or made their way here, surviving whatever hardships were behind or in front of them. Their stories are interesting – as are everyone else's. Sharing is learning.

Here's a more recent and true story about refugees who fled tyranny, and brought their 'foreign ways' with them to Nova Scotia. These are their own words: "In Syria, our passion was to make chocolates. We owned a factory in Damascus for over twenty years. We shipped our specialty treats all over the Middle East. Everything changed when, like much of our homeland, the Hadhad chocolate factory was destroyed in a bombing that forced our family to leave everything behind and flee. Canada was our final destination. With the support of our new Canadian community in Antigonish, and the people of Nova Scotia, we have rebuilt our chocolate company and are once again doing the work we love."

Their company is now called Peace by Chocolate, and its tagline is One peace won't hurt. Their story is printed on the classy box of chocolates I purchased for my research. I learned this: one piece is impossible.

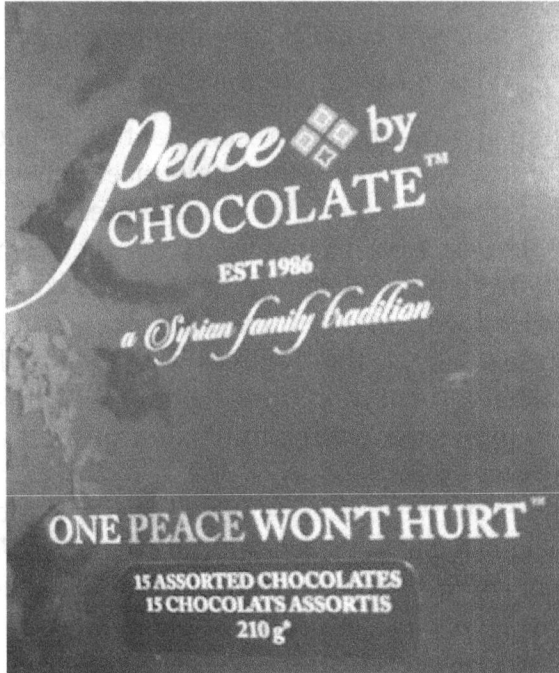

My heart's in the highlands / My heart is not here, wrote Scottish poet Robert Burns. Many Nova Scotians also carry a faraway landscape in their hearts, and we wrestle to accommodate it or adapt.

That's how it is for Lorri Neilsen Glenn, who was born in Winnipeg and grew up in railway towns across Canada. Now a Halifax-based writer and teacher, Lorri sees doppelgangers in landscape.

"When I travel, I often see a scene that reminds me of another place. I wonder, because I have so many roots that are near the sea, the cold, big sky – is something genetic causing me to feel at home here? Or is it just me? I do have the notion that I didn't just plop here by accident. It's complicated," she says. "The western landscape is still in me. I still ache for it sometimes – but when I'm there, I ache for here."

Lorri is a writer, so she naturally searches for the right word to use. "It's a psychic ache, or maybe spiritual – a longing, I guess."

Mrs Lot would understand.

Survey response

Why do I love NS? Because the people are great, the countryside is beautiful, but most of all, I love the ocean, as something to admire, sail on, and just dream beside. I don't want to live anywhere far from the ocean.

Can Nova Scotia provide a satisfactory substitute for the prairie for Lorri? "In Nova Scotia I'm still near a horizon of some kind. Open spaces. Open sky, ocean, a few birds. The ocean is like a prairie sea," she concludes.

Not a coincidence, then, that the windows of her south shore seaside cottage, where a welcome November fire in the grate warms us, offer a wide view of a distant shore, water to the horizon, and big sky.

"My idea of hell would be a crowded city," Lorri says. "I'm out of sorts when I'm in crowded circumstances. I recognize my privilege to be in a place like this while others cannot. I'm lucky and I appreciate that."

As well as finding external landscapes to substitute and satisfy, Lorri found the internal landscape in Nova Scotia to her liking. "I love the community for the sense of proportion here. When we moved to Nova Scotia in the eighties, people here didn't seem to be as driven to capture shiny baubles or achieve status."

I point out that she has both status and baubles: she has a PhD, taught at Mount Saint Vincent University and King's College, was Halifax's poet laureate among many other honours, has published over a dozen books, and shares a home and this cottage with her husband. After a pause, she clarifies: "Here, your friends don't have to be ones that have similar 'assets,' or more social mobility, or are striving not just for a car but for a BMW, or for a large house in the right subdivision. What we have here at this cottage is a retreat, not status. We strove for quality of life."

Later, Lorri emailed more thoughts:

> Victor Frankl's work made me realize why I was so restless in Calgary (my comment about 'strivers' and acquisitiveness, etc). It's all about the search for meaning. Getting material things means nothing unless I'm doing something that I find meaningful (productive, useful, contributing to a community, challenging myself in my writing and teaching). That sounds a whole lot more saintly than I am, but it is true. And it's been my experience that most artists feel the same. The art is meaningful, not the trappings it may afford.

Yes, there is an echo in Lorri's words. Maybe it's Tina Hennigar, inviting people to Lunenburg County's lifestyle boom. Or Sandee MacLean in Whycocomagh: "We should promote our small community lifestyle, but we don't. There's the impression that people who choose to live here are not very smart. You can go away and earn big money, but big money usually goes with big debt."

By the way, Sandee MacLean's Facebook post, offering two acres of land, a job at the Farmer's Daughter Country Market, and quality of life, received well over three hundred thousand responses. In 2019, the Cape Breton Partnership launched a website to help respond to this tsunami of interest in opportunities in little Whycocomagh and all of Cape Breton.

In comparison, the 'bump' in the number of visits to the Cape Breton tourism website right after a divisive US election was an also-extraordinary twenty-five thousand. Both are evidence that thousands of people the world over are dreaming of a home and life like what they perceive we have in Nova Scotia.

The unthinkable

I have a theory that we tend to match events to the landscape in which they occur. For example, we expect poverty in a tenement, rats in an alley, bombs in war zones, and sweet people in a beautiful countryside. More and more, it seems that events are occurring in places not meant for them, such as child abuse in residential schools, and mass murders in places of worship. Trouble is not staying in its lane, but perhaps it never did. Our world view is changing as we experience new miseries. Trouble doesn't just happen down south or overseas. It happens very close to home. Too close.

In the spring of 2020, Nova Scotia was joined to the whole world in a pandemic. We had to refresh our understanding of what the word even meant, in theory and in practice. Surely, not here?

Our provincial government decreed measures to protect Nova Scotians from the potential ravages of the Covid-19 virus. We were ordered, in our Premier's gruff words, to "stay the blazes home!" So we did. Some of us felt fortunate that our homes were the designated refuge from this new threat, that staying inside and watching TV would save our lives, unlike when the threat is fire or flood and you have to flee from your home. It took a bit of getting used to, but we were doing it.

Then, the unthinkable.

A small community on the stunningly beautiful shores of the Bay of Fundy was thrust into the national spotlight and the record books for being ground zero of "the worst mass murder in Canadian history." In their homes or out for a Sunday morning walk or running to help a neighbour, twenty-two innocent people were murdered in cold blood. At home.

Widespread shock and grief pushed pandemic concerns aside, for a moment. The Nova Scotia Song, already melancholy, became a lament. Because of restrictions against congregating to prevent transmission of the virus, mourners were not permitted to gather, nor families to grieve together, and no funerals were held.

Days later, a helicopter accompanying the HMCS Fredericton out of Halifax mysteriously crashed into the Ionian Sea where it was on NATO manoeuvres, killing all six of its crew. Three of the six were Nova Scotians, but Nova Scotia is home for all crew who sail out of the harbour.

"What next?" we asked, though we didn't want an answer. Meanwhile, the invisible virus was quietly dispatching dozens of our beloved elders, and forcing us all to continue to stay home, where prolonged isolation threatened the safety and mental health of many.

But an answer did come. A period of heavy spring rains, swelling a town stream, may have created a fascinating and deadly attraction for a little boy. At the time of this writing, only his rubber boots had been found.

Multiple losses are hard to comprehend, but the mental image of those little boots gets to the heart of grief.

As succeeding miserable events unfolded, we said, "We'll get through this. We've survived disaster before."

It's true. Here are just a very few of the disasters this beautiful province has seen:

- 1998: Swissair Flight 111 crash: all 229 passengers and crew died
- 1992: Westray Mine: 26 miners died

- 1958: Springhill Mine: 75 miners died
- 1956: Springhill Mine: 39 miners died
- 1917: New Waterford Mine: 62 miners died
- 1917: Halifax Explosion, 2000 citizens died
- 1891: Springhill Mine: 125 miners died
- 1873: SS *Atlantic* shipwreck: 565 passengers and crew died

I haven't included the thousands of fatalities in historic declared wars, or murders in undeclared conflicts, in our shared history. I haven't included the countless fishermen and others lost at sea, nor the estimated five thousand shipwrecks on our shores.

The tendency, as I suggested earlier, is to say that tragedy doesn't belong here: we're too nice, or too small, or the scenery is just too beautiful to permit it. We want to believe that misery belongs in faraway places where we imagine that the citizens are accustomed to it, and accept it.

That can't be true. Whether it's a legend of a tyrannical deity or a present-day tyrant raining destruction on innocent people, nobody can become accustomed to that. Everyone wishes for a long and peaceful life, maybe making chocolates or raising sheep. Nova Scotia is a great place to do that. We don't want our communities to be known as that place where that awful thing happened.

Whether in small or large numbers, these losses of life can be almost incomprehensible. We try to put them into context. We've spent centuries comforting ourselves with the thought that the fishermen, miners, military, and others we lost must have known the risks. The thing is, a risk is not a probability. Nobody goes to work expecting to come home in a box or not at all. Nobody expects, while sheltering at home from an easily-avoided virus, to be killed there by a bullet.

Nova Scotians have grieved at each of these terrible events, past and present. We may know someone involved, given the few degrees of separation in this small place. But even as we grieve, we don't expect the same thing to happen again tomorrow. We are not at war, and are not in a high crime area. Our homes are safe. Our communities are safe. The unthinkable may happen again, whether by a madman or maybe climate change, but for most of us, most of the time, life is quiet here. We should not be of two minds about that. Water will continue to flow under the bridge, and little children will always be drawn to the slippery banks.

People, seeking

I'm struck by the similarities with, and differences between, the experience of those disenfranchised Scots on the *Hector* in the 18th century and the appeal for new settlers in Whycocomagh in the 21st century. Punishment versus opportunity. Betrayal versus a fair deal. Interests of the crown versus interests of the community. People seeking a satisfying and secure home centuries apart.

Not everyone stuck it out or survived the challenge in either century, but at least we behave more humanely toward newcomers now.

"We have quality of life," echoes Pam Mood. "The ocean, the land, the arts, what else – the people. People are second to none. You come as strangers, you stay as friends. Everyone is family to us. It has been said of Nova Scotians that we are friendly but not welcoming. Well, that's not the case in Yarmouth, not any more."

Eric Hustvedt in Broad Cove, too: "One reason I never felt the need to move anywhere else is the landscape here, the variety of things to see and do, the different cultures and heritages within short drives of here. There's a friendly atmosphere. Maybe the Buddhists were onto something."

In 1976, a Buddhist leader led hundreds of his flock to Nova Scotia from Boulder, Colorado, having found something special about this place. Many remain to this day.

"Having a local gathering place, a café – where people know your name – that helps," Eric continues. "We have to entertain ourselves. Some don't have a whole lot – we don't. Sometimes we had to take multiple jobs to be able to survive here."

Eric Hustvedt and Phyllis Price aren't complaining, just explaining that being able to stay and live in their Broad Cove home has been worth the effort it took.

I imagine Lorri Neilsen Glenn, Winnipeg-born, and Pam Mood, Yarmouth-born, would enjoy sitting on a seaside bench with Lydia Adams, Glace Bay-born, for a big sky chat. "Living by the ocean is so powerful," Lydia says. "It's a tremendous force to live beside: the pull, the ebb and flow, the unending sky."

Or maybe they wouldn't talk; maybe they'd just share the moment in friendly silence beside the expanse of salt water.

Survey response

Home is waking up to seagulls laughing and the aroma of lingering tides. Home is the feeling that greeted me at the door of the old family homestead, with weathered floorboards and memories creaking underfoot.
Home is traditions and superstitions...

Not everyone in Nova Scotia lives with rural or coastal scenery. Taking into account all the residents of Nova Scotia's two urban centres (Halifax and Sydney) and the twenty-six towns, you've got more than half the province's population living where there are street lights at night, where somebody will deliver a pizza or Chinese food to your door on a Saturday night if you want, and many more diversions and amenities beckon.

The rest of the population is scattered around little hamlets, adorable or otherwise, down gravel roads and up steep hills and out on rocky promontories, where residents deal with things that urbanites might not think of, including septic tanks. They fight to keep their roads paved or plowed, fight to keep their bridges safe, fight to keep their schools open, fight for ferry and ambulance service, fight for internet and cellphone signals, fight for minority representation in government, fight for doctors – okay, everyone's doing that. They fight against clear-cutting, fracking, quarries, fish

119

farms, wind turbines (if nearby), landfills, mills, mines, and any other development or industry that would disturb or destroy their quiet enjoyment of their homes.

They put on their parkas and join worldwide movements in marching down their narrow, shoulderless roads to protest the ignorance pandemic. They have few or no streetlights. They might fight against those, too: light pollution is a thing, and people in cities and towns can't see the awesome Milky Way because of it.

And of course there are the spring peepers, so celebrated when they first appear. If you don't know what they are, ask someone in the country to tell you. You'll have a lovely conversation. Hint: they're not flowers.

Two Hearts, Two Homes?
By S. B. Borgersen

There is a saying, 'home is where the heart is' – but hearts can be like stomachs, can't they? For instance I know a guy who assures me we all have two stomachs: one for the main course, and one for dessert. So do we have two hearts: one for the place we want to be and the people we want to be with (the main course) and the other for the loved ones left behind in the places we were rooted (dessert)?

It's an interesting subject and it was the main focus of a discussion group (interestingly, all poets) I was invited to participate in a few years ago. Those present were ... people who had discovered the Maritimes and recognized the area for its gentleness and kindness of its people, its unpolluted air and its unique culture and support of the arts.

I listened as each person around the circle spoke of HOME and what it meant to them. And then it was my turn. I explained how I had come here [from Britain] for a long weekend in the 1980s. It was February, minus 28 Celsius. The Bay was frozen over. I was overwhelmed with the natural beauty of the area and the warmth of the people. How, in the three short days of my visit, I'd decided this is where I wanted to be. How, after years of being a 'camp follower' to my first husband's work, I had found a place that would stop me 'following'.

I told them I had lived here, in our 1898 forever-in-need-of-repair home, longer than I have lived anywhere. And that I had no intention of leaving. How I had applied for Canadian citizenship and how it took eight years to be awarded that honour.

It was a major turning point in my life, one of many as it turns out. I gave up all I knew in the UK: house, mortgage, career, family nearby, theatre, restaurants, boutiques – do you want the entire list? And I came to a place where a night out was to stand on the headland and gaze at the moon over the ocean. Where a new designer outfit for a party came, with great excitement I might add, from the local thrift store for a dollar (and could be donated back a week later so someone else could dress up for a party and the Salvation Army would benefit from true recycling).

I learned to do without some of those familiar, take-them-for-granted items, especially groceries: Oxo cubes, Roses lime marmalade, plain flour. Slowly over time I found they were not important. Well, you can't top a friendly neighbour turning up on the doorstep with fresh lobster, or halibut or haddock. Or the brother-in-law's home-smoked, locally caught salmon eaten in big meaty chunks instead of wafer thin slices.

But for a long time, 'home' was still back there in England. It was part of my dialogue, as in, 'back home we do this, or that.' I had bouts of homesickness; that craving for family, history, roots, and a great Indian meal. England was still my 'main course heart' and Nova Scotia, my adopted home, was still my 'dessert'.

The time when, without thinking, I knew where home truly was, occurred on one of my annual trips to England to visit family and friends a few years ago. It happened as I was saying goodbye. I checked in at Heathrow airport, breathing a sigh of relief, and waving to familiar faces in the Air Canada departure lounge. I understood at that very moment: yes, I was leaving behind people and places I loved, but I was also leaving behind a lifestyle that had become alien to me. I was on my way back to Nova Scotia, following my 'main course heart' to the place I wanted to be.

I was on my way home.

5 – Where or What is Home for You?

> *Survey responses*
>
> *When I lived away, I longed for home, not really understanding what that meant. Something / many things were missing, and even after I returned, the vacancies in my soul remained. It took several years of being back in the province before I found home.*
>
> <>
>
> *Home now is where my husband and I bought a house and purposely put down roots. No matter where I travel, knowing that I have this "home base" makes all the difference. So...my house is my home, the place where my husband, my cat and my art studio reside.*

Trusting your compass

"Do you know where you're going to? Do you like the things that life is showing you?" asks the theme song from the 1975 movie *Mahogany*. My twenty-eight interviews and one hundred surveys did not reveal one common answer to these musical questions, no singular factor that everyone needs or wants in order to feel at home.

Having meaningful work; feeling welcome inside and outside your door; looking at the combination of land, water, and sky that suits your eye; being mindful of others' need to feel welcome and how we're able to make that happen; wanting to make friends or to live a solitary life – these and more are aspects of some happy lives, and by extension, some happy homes.

But not all.

Some people don't feel at home everywhere, but do when in a specific social community, like Vanessa Fells who began in

Yarmouth and has her eye on global issues. Some are happy if the external landscape matches their interior one, like prairie girl Lorri Nielsen Glenn.

Some know they're home but must strive to restore its essence, like Mi'kmaq Jessie Hatt or French instructor Beverly Hugli. Others just know when they're in the right place, like Jay LeBlanc on her father's land, and Judith Varney Burch, and me.

Some work to improve their home communities, like Mayor Pam Mood and enterpriser and philanthropist Annette Verschuren. Many feel the community around them offers all they need, like homebody Kathy Rafuse and local champions Tina Hennigar and Sandee MacLean.

Immigration executive Jennifer Watts and curious neighbour Kacy Petersen Delong know that welcoming newcomers makes them feel at home, too. Councillor Eric Hustvedt and community engager Phyllis Price worked extra jobs to be able to stay where they chose as their home, and to ensure opportunity would be there for others, as did milliner Anna Shoub.

Some encountered discomforts while searching for comforts that matter, like physician Krishna Srivatsa, artist Brandt Eisner, and lawyer Veryan Haysom. Some find home in their art, like quilt artist Valerie Hearder, rug-hooker Deanne Fitzpatrick, and conductor Lydia Adams.

Teachers Lloyd and Maude Bailey will roll wherever life takes them. Professor Liz Smith and businessman Robert Smith, from the east and west coasts, are at home in the American south where the stork delivered their child. Helping others feel welcome works for retired teacher Greg Selig and marathon runner and cyclist Janis Power.

When you're searching for home, you might find a compass useful. It's a simple device, just a magnetic bar balanced on a pin, aligned with the earth's magnetic lines. While Canada's national anthem sings of the true north, that's more poetry than fact. Navigators learn that a compass doesn't point to True north, but to Magnetic north, which is high on the Canadian map but always moving southward. The difference between those norths is called

Variation. There may also be magnetic items near the compass, distracting the wobbly arrow, causing Deviation.

As helmsman, you know to 'always trust your compass,' but only after the navigator (likely also you) has calculated for TVMDC: True - Variation - Magnetic - Deviation - Compass. After also calculating for wind and current, you should be able to plot your course confidently toward your home port.

In other words, the magnet may be simple (the pull, the desire), but the journey and choice of destination are complicated.

After all that, your safe arrival in a port is no guarantee that it's the port of your dreams. Perhaps it seemed like it would be when you started out or were being tossed around on the briny ocean. But your experiences once you have arrived may not be to your liking. Any port in a storm is a popular saying, but storms never last, and when fair weather returns you may choose to move on.

And then there are happy accidents. One day, I was sailing in one of Nova Scotia's beautiful bays when I spied another boat of the same make and model. As any sailor knows, two similar boats sailing in the same direction constitutes a race. We quickly declared an island beach as our destination and the race was on. The other boat pulled ahead, closing in on the wharf where he would tie up and run to the beach.

These boats had centreboards, so I sailed straight for the beach, raised the centreboard at the last minute, dropped the sails, and slid to a halt on the sand. I jumped out and declared my boat the winner.

An old man and his grandson came toward us. The old man asked with concern, "I just wanted to know, did you mean to do that?"

He was sure he had witnessed a shipwreck, which it might have been but for all the celebrating on the beach. Some arrivals are like that. But we weren't home.

Home isn't just one place or thing, because we are not one thing. Whether home is people or a place or a feeling or a combination, it is subject to far-away variations and close-by deviations in the same way all our affections and aspirations are.

Being welcoming and feeling welcomed both depend to a very large degree on our ability to make friends. That's why the experiences of 'sticking out and fitting in' described earlier were so similar for new and old residents alike.

Knowing home

Survey response

Place plays a big part in 'home' but so do the people. It's a combination of both. One without the other would not be at all the same. Familiar experiences play a role, too.

I wonder if our fondness for a hometown or attachment to a landscape can be compared to our feelings for cherished family pets. We give them untrammelled affection and feel it is reciprocated. It's not easy to move on from those feelings after our favoured animals die, even if we replace them with new animal companions.

Our affections for humans are deep too, of course, but far more complex. We cherish some people in our hearts for life, while we may try to forget entirely the troublesome memory of others.

So too, our affection for a land which has not betrayed us should receive its due. It's not 'just a place' if we have loved it.

And even after we've found home, our thinking about it may still evolve.

As we wrap up our conversation in the Halifax mall food court, Jennifer Watts is still musing. "What do I feel is home? I think my perspective is changing somewhat," she says. "With the growing awareness of First Nations' historic possession of the land, and of our heritage as settlers, and working with refugees who have had to flee their homeland which they may have loved and valued, I ask why I feel such a strong attachment to place – to this place – and whether that is appropriate. Perhaps I'm learning not to take 'place' for granted."

For many, home doesn't include land ownership and doesn't need to, but access to the land around us is important and a feature of life in Nova Scotia. In the centre of peninsular Halifax is a large green space called The Common. Back in the mid-1700s, when this book's accounts began, the British king granted this 235-acre common 'for the use of the inhabitants of the town of Halifax forever.'

Now, less than one-third of the original grant is still open land, with public buildings and a cemetery on the rest. A parking garage was proposed for some of the remaining green space which a politician said was not being 'used.'

Nova Scotia has so much land that is not 'used', that is, doesn't have crowds of people on it all the time; that's not the point of wilderness or urban parks. Easy access to beaches, lakes, parks and rocky shores brings a lot of pleasure to many Nova Scotians, whether we live down a gravel road or up an elevator. Citizens must rally ever more frequently to defend old growth forests against clear-cutting, pristine waters against fish farms, wilderness areas from golf course developments, and Canada's oldest urban park from parking garages.

These issues affect residents deeply, and can shake our confidence in our home communities and those we elect to take care of our public assets. Feeling secure where we live and shop and walk the dog can make or break our sense of home.

Feeling welcomed helps, too. A friendly smile, a wave, are not expensive to give and we should not dole them out as though they are.

On a visit to my doctor's clinic, a medical student carefully removed a bandage. She spoke with an accent different from mine, so I asked where she was from.

"From Iraq," she said, a little hesitantly, perhaps unsure of my reaction.

"You're a long way from home," I said. "Thank you for coming to Nova Scotia. We need doctors here." Judging by her smile, I think I made her day.

> *Survey response*
>
> *Home is a place that provides a person with the things that have been important to him/her over the years. Home satisfies a need, makes us happy, offers freedom or protection, or is unique in some way; for example, in helping us develop our talents, feelings and beliefs.*

While I was gathering material for this book, I attended four events at which I was more or less an outsider, and which I might not have attended if I wasn't researching my own impressions, looking for my 'discomfort zone:'

July: Sailing on the Bras d'Or Lake out of Baddeck:

The University of Cape Breton sponsored the cruise to celebrate an honorary degree recipient. The Chancellor of UCB is Annette Verschuren, a busy woman who suggested I interview her on board to save time. However, the scenery, food, music, and people are too pleasantly distracting for work, so we agree to meet again the next morning for our discussion.

September: The New Germany Community Pot-luck Supper:
Seated in my folding chair in the grassy area under the maples along New Germany's Main Street, I recognize six people, including Greg Selig, who had invited me to the event when we talked in July at Kejimkujik National Park. The Lion's Club Train is transporting happy children along the trail behind us. When we hear "Supper's ready!" we form a queue at a long table to help ourselves to salads, meats and hot dogs, followed by portions of a large Canada 150 cake.

November: South Shore Refugee Family Reunification meeting, Mahone Bay:
I recognize four people. A local radio personality begins the meeting by announcing that we are on un-ceded Mi'kmaq territory. We learn that the project must raise $52,000 to bring eight relatives of a local Syrian family to Canada and support them for one year. Kacy Petersen DeLong of Barss Corner outlines tasks needing volunteers. Refreshments are coffee and 'Syrian cookies.'

December: The Cornwall Baptist Church children's Christmas concert:
Proud relatives of the little ones, who perform like rock stars, fill the church. I know Kathy Rafuse at the piano. I'm heading to another event so I dash out early – nearly knocking over Santa Claus who is waiting behind the door to make his grand entrance. I tell him I've been good, which seems to surprise him.

My analysis: My comfort level or sense of belonging at these events varied, but it was because of what I like to do, not because of the people who invited me or who I recognized there. I like each of them, and each welcomed me. As Sandee MacLean, Deanne Fitzpatrick, and Phyllis Price said, you can't integrate into a community unless you get out and get involved. Showing up is just the first step.

For certain, nobody said they didn't want me there, or told me I should go back where I came from, or pulled their purses close when I walked by, as people of colour often experience. I didn't expect they would, of course; that would be absurd. It's always absurd.

When Lydia Adams tours with her choir she creates home wherever she goes, not only for herself, but for whoever attends. She herself is the newcomer in the cities and towns, but she sees it as her mission to make the audience feel welcome in her concerts and workshops; to not be intimidated by these 'really good' singers, but to feel welcome in their midst; to invite people to hear music that might be unfamiliar, but which they might come to love.

Can we do that, on our own stages, in our daily performances? Jennifer Watts in Halifax told me about a foot race, possibly during the Blue Nose Marathon series that draws some 12,000 runners of all ages. The volunteer who shouted "Good job!" to a runner at the finish line was a newcomer to Canada. It was reportedly a moving moment and a new perspective for that runner.

I bet that volunteer didn't feel like an outsider while making tired runners happy to see him.

The chocolate-makers in Antigonish who say 'one peace won't hurt' are creating a new home for themselves by helping us to be happy (if fine chocolate makes you happy). They may still grieve for what they lost in Damascus – why wouldn't they? – but going back seems a very remote option, especially since they now have a successful business employing fifty-five of their new neighbours. Perhaps they're still of two minds about settling in Nova Scotia. They do seem determined to find happiness here, just like the fabled traveller seemed to the old man, and that might help take the noise of the bombings out of their ears.

> *Survey response*
>
> *This province is one of the most beautiful places in the world. My father was from England and my parents travelled extensively, but they never found any place better to live. Every place has its problems, and people seem to be all too willing to focus on those instead of the good that is here. Let's focus on the good and maybe our fortunes will start turning around.*

To 'focus on the good' sounds nice, seems like the right thing to say, but the good must be good for everyone, and not a reason to ignore problems or accept the status quo.

In her book, Cape Bretoner Annette Verschuren offers the powerful mantra, "Not bad, not good, only better." Take the bad with the good, she says, but focus on doing better.

In other words, as poet Maya Angelou said, "Do the best you can until you know better. Then, when you know better, do better."

We know better now than the settlers did hundreds of years ago, and we can surely do better at being welcoming to all now.

When all Nova Scotians enjoy the same basic qualities of life, nobody loses, everybody wins. A rising tide floats all ships.

"Where's home?" is a perpetual question, whether the question ends 'for me' or 'for you.' Seeking its answers helps us learn about ourselves and our neighbours. Let's keep asking.

> ...place is many things for me, much more than a horizon, set of hills, quality of light, or familiar road.[...]It is a moving, personal force of the mind and heart with a complex, evolving geography that goes beyond its latitude and longitude on the planet.
>
> -- from **Threading Light** by Lorri Neilsen Glenn

Jan Fancy Hull

Afterthoughts – the Bad, the Good, and the Better

Where's Home? recently sat down with author Jan Fancy Hull for an unusual self-interview.

Where's Home: I am your first non-fiction book, and the publisher is preparing me for launch as we speak. Congratulations. You must be very happy.

Jan Fancy Hull: Thank you. I'm thrilled to have found Moose House Publications. They focus on publishing books about, or written in, rural Nova Scotia. I appreciate that and hope this book will repay the attention they are bringing to us. I am quite happy.

WH: I sense a hesitation. What is it?

JFH: You are very perceptive. I was pleased with the project all the way through the process: the interviews, selecting the anonymous comments, helping to share stories about the many ways Nova Scotians experience life in or away from this province. I think I honoured the trust my interview subjects placed in me to relate their experiences. I do like how I wove it all together, and added the contributed poems and blogs *et cetera* to illustrate some points. But something didn't sit right with me, something felt out of balance. I needed to explore what that was.

WH: And did you find it?

JFH: Yes, eventually. You see, my aim was to create a book that would not be a replica of other books about Nova Scotia, nor easily pigeon-holed. I didn't set out to write an ode to New Scotland's hills and glens, though when people mentioned such things, I put them in. Nor did I want to assemble a reference book that was all facts and dates, though I included some when they seemed pertinent. I envisioned the book as a broad conversation which I hoped would spark other conversations beyond its covers, that would open a topic and poke it a bit, but not poke so hard that people wouldn't continue to read. There's raising a subject, and there's preaching. One must go lightly.

WH: Well, I think you nailed it.

JFH: You would.

WH: So where's your problem?

JFH: Right at the end. I selected a few great quotes to finish with, including a gentle admonishment from Maya Angelou to 'do better'. Perfect. But what nagged at me was that last comment from an anonymous survey respondent. Here it is again:

> This province is one of the most beautiful places in the world...Every place has its problems, and people seem to be all too willing to focus on those instead of the good that is here. Let's focus on the good and maybe our fortunes will start turning around.

WH: I saw that. You did comment on it. You said To 'focus on the good' sounds nice, seems like the right thing to say, but the good must be good for everyone, and not a reason to ignore problems or accept the status quo.

JFH: I realized that I need to press harder on that platitude. The more I thought about it, the more I heard a lifetime of people telling me to focus on the good. Telling someone to focus on the good is shutting them down. It is saying, 'Don't criticize, that's not polite. Don't complain, you sound ungrateful.' It silences people who may be trying to express legitimate concerns.

WH: That happened to you?

JFH: Oh, sure, lots of times, when I was growing up. At home, in church, at school. At work. All anyone in authority had to do was utter some platitude like that and my genie was stuffed back in the bottle. 'Respect your elders' and 'Count your blessings' are two more of that ilk. Also what Thumper said, you know: 'If you can't say anything nice, don't say anything at all.' By the time I was thirty, I didn't need anyone to say it to me, I said it to myself — and probably to others. Maybe I didn't focus on the good, but I learned to be quiet, to not rock the boat. To 'go along to get along,' as someone said in one of my interviews. I did get along, but progress was difficult and slow. I could have done better for myself and my employers, but they didn't want to hear from 'the girl.'

WH: Ugh. And later? Did it get better?

JFH: Yes it did, probably starting around the time I turned fifty. I began to realize that I didn't need someone else's approval to govern my own opinion of me, that my perspectives are important, too. That doesn't mean I was suddenly self-assured and outspoken, oh no; old habits die hard. But they have faded. I'm much older now. And more confident.

WH: You don't focus on the good now?

JFH: I hadn't really thought about it until I put that statement at the end of the book. Nobody has tried to lay that platitude on me for some time. Perhaps it's because I can choose to be in situations now where I have, or appear to have, confidence and/or authority. Which makes my point: we tend to shut down people of differing viewpoints if they don't have the agency to argue back. So minority voices need to be protected.

WH: Interesting point. What do you do?

JFH: Personally? I try to focus on problems and solutions. If there's a challenge or an obstacle in my way, I don't ignore it or give up, I get up. I try to see how I can take that sad song and make it better, to focus on what's possible. I quite enjoy trying to work things out. In stone sculpture, of which I am a practitioner, that's pretty much the whole job right there. Problem (or opportunity) = chunk of stone. Possibilities = design. Strategy = tools and time. Solution = sculpture. If I focus on a problem long enough, asking why it is a problem and for whom, and seeking ways to resolve it, the fix is in.

WH: You must accomplish a lot.

JFH: I don't mean to suggest that I'm successful at everything I try. Sometimes I can't see ahead, but the plan works most times. Focusing only on the good is blindness, whether wilful or otherwise. I've taken on some projects that I was told were hopeless, with little good left to focus on. To me, those situations simply suffered from a failure of imagination. 'Tools and time,' by the way, is a quote from a little stone carving book I discovered years ago. The author asked a man who was displaying his set of jade chess pieces, "How did you make them?" "Tools and time," was his simple reply. You might say he neglected to mention technique or artistic vision, but I believe he knew that those aspects manifest while you patiently apply your tools. Baroque composer JS Bach said that anyone could write the music he wrote if they were willing to work as hard as he did, meaning to put in the time with the tools. Einstein celebrated imagination. None of those men, nor any other person in the history of any worthy accomplishment, claimed to simply focus on the good while hoping things would change by themselves. Instead, I know they focused on the possible, all day long, to create the change they wanted.

WH: Having made that point, are you more comfortable with the tone of this book?

JFH: Somewhat. Even though I've said that focusing on the good is license to ignore the bad, I think it happens in the book.

WH: I don't think you've ignored the bad. People mentioned many uncomfortable aspects of life in Nova Scotia, and your method was to follow their lead, right?

JFH: Right. The format allowed me to address some touchy topics, but I still wonder if I may have glossed over them.

WH: You're being your book's first critic.

JFH: Maybe. Before it goes to print, though, I can add my weight here to some messages in the book, which is preferable to inserting my opinion into an individual's story. That might have been putting words in their mouth, or interrupted the flow of the conversation. There are some great conversations in it.

WH: So what is something you want to re-balance?

JFH: Racism. I interviewed one African Nova Scotian woman, and reported her account of the town cops telling her and her sister they were not wanted in their neighbourhood when they were kids. That's a hurtful story, but to them, it's not a story: it's their lived experience. What good should they focus on? When I saw that photo of those little girls, giggling together, my heart broke. Who hurts children? If there is good in that story – and I see none –

it is far outweighed by the deliberate and ugly harm aimed at children because of the colour of their skin.

WH: Nobody should argue with that, but I suppose some do.

JFH: Many do. But compare: I was born into a working-class white family. I've been able to earn a good living. If luck is defined as preparation meeting opportunity, I've been lucky many times. I had great adventures and still do. I am comfortable in whatever community I call home. Nova Scotians of African descent can never count on any of that. They can't just focus on the good. In the book, I created imaginary scenarios where people I interviewed would sit on a bench by the sea or at a table in a café and just enjoy their shared love of place or high-five their agreements. Although I know each person I interviewed would welcome anyone at that table or bench, I think African Nova Scotians can never be certain of that.

WH: Some Nova Scotians might say people who feel excluded may be excluding themselves.

JFH: I'm guessing that they would be people who haven't had to live with the glances and the whispers, being passed over for jobs, or being stopped by the police for walking while Black. Or maybe they just never thought about it long enough to walk in others' shoes. Here's a story of discrimination they might relate to more personally: one of the anonymous survey responses tells of their family moving into a community where the incoming Protestant girls were told to stay away from the resident Catholic boys. Two problems there: ostracism due to religious beliefs, and blaming girls for what the boys want to do. Those practices are pervasive, destructive, and not just a feature of the 'bad old days'. Focusing on the good only drives the harm underground.

WH: Why not just come right out and say that racism or discrimination of any kind is wrong?

JFH: It's been said. And I do know that African Nova Scotians, or 'Africadians,' to use the term that Nova Scotian author George Elliott Clarke coined, don't want or need me to speak for them.

WH: But you can say how you feel. That's valid, right?

JFH: It sure is, and I'm doing that now. Another way is to quote someone who says what I want said. My book is filled with opinions spoken by the people I interviewed plus a hundred other anonymous survey respondents, and they do carry a lot of weight. I also can paraphrase what the late African-American writer Toni Morrison said: if you're racist, there's something mentally wrong with you and you should seek help for it. I love that she said it — that hating another person because of the colour of their skin is not just wrong, it's an illness. Let's declare racism to be an epidemic and develop some treatment facilities for people with that condition so they won't infect others.

WH: That's novel.

JFH: No it isn't. Do you remember the woman I interviewed who told her kids that if they couldn't find something good about everyone in their village there was something wrong with them – the kids? It is that simple. She taught her children well.

WH: Speaking on behalf of other people's experiences is a bit patronizing.

JFH: It's a lot patronizing. I'm learning. We now know that Black or Indigenous people don't appreciate white people writing stories as them. I say 'now,' because we had to be told. They can represent themselves very well. White people tend to see the world from the white point of view. And we tend to think we know how everything goes and what's best for everyone else. I know I can't speak about how people must feel when discriminated against because of their race, but I can speak on behalf of myself. So I say this: racism carried out on my behalf, by government and law enforcement at any level, is an abuse of the power which I, as a citizen, give them. And I say this is not how I want things to be done in my home. Whoever stands up and says, "Yes, but look at all the good..." can just sit down.

WH: Does that resolve your conflicts with the balance of this book?

JFH: There's more. I realized that the history I was taught in school was distorted. Perhaps the dates of battles were accurate, but the whys and wherefores of them were definitely told from the point of view of the victors, meaning the British settlers and their descendants. A call to focus on the good implies that everyone should just appreciate the inventions and innovations that have been achieved in the last few centuries. Democratic government. Roads. Universal suffrage. Universal health care. Electricity. Internet. Clean drinking water.

WH: What's wrong with that?

JFH: Nothing, except not everyone who calls this place home has them to enjoy, or not in equal measure. Indigenous peoples had to walk a fine line between the French and the British who settled their ancestral lands. They negotiated treaties in good faith, but those treaties were not honoured, not then and not still. So Indigenous people are marching and blockading, protesting the usurping and destruction of their territories, the impoverishment of their people, the ruination of their – our – natural resources. Those protesters don't have millions to lose. They just want to be lifted out of poverty.

WH: Not all First Nations people are in agreement, though.

JFH: Is that a surprise? Why expect Indigenous people to be unified when the settlers did everything they could to take away their power, language, families, health, and dignity? To those who point out all the good we 'gave' them, I say: we took their land and nearly their souls. If we want to list who got what, we must be fair. But we don't need to make lists. We just need to make sure that all our citizens enjoy the benefits of this province, equally. Without having to boil their well water. I said in the early part of the book that Nova Scotia's history is our shared history. We can't cherry-pick the bits we like and romanticize or blame the rest away. As Dalhousie University says, we are all treaty people. History can't be undone, but it can play out better for everyone.

WH: I see why you didn't put these comments in the text of the book. You wove the stories for readers to interpret as they will, but now you want to make sure they know where you stand.

JFH: It's not just about where I stand, either, but where this book stands. I know the power of the written word. The book will speak for itself long after it's published. I want it to give readers a broad look into the many ways people experience home in Nova Scotia (or anywhere, I expect), and why some are unable to achieve the comfort and confidence they are entitled to.

WH: You've done that now.

JFH: I have more. What about LGBTQ+ people? Who can honestly say that being anywhere on the sexual orientation bell-curve is a choice? To whom does it make sense that a child or adult would choose a life of marginalization, to live as an object of derision and alienation by family, teachers, church leaders, or anyone with a half-baked opinion of how they live?

WH: Sure, but this is wide-spread. Nova Scotians aren't the only ones who —

JFH: There you go! Don't we love to say we're not as bad as people somewhere else. That doesn't excuse us for discriminating or promoting hate, not one time, not ever. We are proud whenever a Nova Scotian achieves something of importance. Why not announce that we have all decided to embrace inclusiveness, province-wide? And do it?

WH: That won't happen. Some people don't feel comfortable being inclusive of all lifestyles.

JFH: Personal discomfort is no excuse for harming others or holding them down. That's why I wanted to make my position clear: that I do not endorse homophobia, racism, sexism, or discrimination of any sort. I may not be 'woke' to all the ways they happen, and I may say or do offensive things myself unawares, but that doesn't mean I think it's okay. I find myself editing what I say all the time, as I realize that what I used to say was or could be hurtful. It's no hardship. It doesn't cost me anything to give someone else a little comfort. The cynics call that 'political correctness.' It's not. It's human kindness.

WH: Aren't you woke? Isn't this interview evidence of that?

JFH: Not really. Woke refers to a heightened awareness of injustices, especially racial. I doubt I would be considered woke by anyone who fights in that arena. But I have created this book, which touches on historic and current social and racial injustices, and I want to make sure my book's compass is pointing in the right direction by eliminating as much local deviation as possible. One of the things that makes social change (or any change) so difficult is well-intentioned people who think they already know what's wrong and what should be done about it, and that there should be nothing more to learn or to say on the subject. I want to stay aware of my lack of awareness, while keeping my eyes and ears open. Checking my privilege, in other words.

WH: We cover many other topics.

JFH: We do. Language. Religion. People from away. It's my perception that we are a little more open to newcomers here than we used to be, though I can't speak for those who experience personal difficulties. That's what the book illustrates, I hope. The answer to 'Where's home for you?' is always personal, because home is an individual concept. So if someone experiences home here in a way that is different from mine, I should not suggest they focus on the good. My good may not be their good.

WH: We talk about people who feel at home on the land or near the ocean.

JFH: Yes, including me. Thanks for reminding me about another imbalance I don't want to gloss over. We are truly blessed with the scenery in Nova Scotia. Scenery is not some intangible concept, or without value. Our clean air is an attraction that thousands of tourists spend millions of much-appreciated dollars to experience. That is a 'good' that we can focus on, but not blindly, not while the government permits forests to be clear-cut so severely that the trees will not return in our lifetimes, and never again with the biodiversity they supported. The money made from such carnage will quickly go down the road while erosion and floods will leave their destructive mark forever on this home we cherish.

WH: That's disturbing.

JFH: It seems that we keep electing governments that can't think of any way to bring prosperity to this province other than to cut trees to the ground. Even forest fires leave less devastation. And if there's a green space in the big city, which most cities in the world yearn for, it is considered a prime site for a parking garage. I don't like conspiracy theories or general distrust of our politicians, but they do give us new reasons daily why we should be on guard, that we must always ask "Who benefits?" from what they propose. We can make a list of the good things we have, but not to watch them disappear.

WH: At least the tides still roll in.

JFH: Oh, the ocean is another battle-ground.

WH: You mean all the plastic in the ocean? Isn't that everywhere?

JFH: Two things. First: fish farms in our bays. It seems most folk who live near them don't want them, but the government doesn't heed. "Jobs" is the flag behind which so much harm marches into our communities. The jobs often don't appear, or if they do, they are rarely as plentiful or well-paying as promised, not for the hopeful locals. If it all goes wrong and the business closes, those jobs and the businesses that grew up around them are gone. Communities and hearts and families are broken. And we, the taxpayers, are left to foot the bill for the damages. Some people I interviewed suggested that the government should stop pouring millions into big businesses, and help unique local enterprises to thrive instead.

WH: People need work.

JFH: Of course they do. We need the kind of businesses that attract handfuls of talented families and workers to communities where they will make a difference and have a good life. Small enterprises are the bedrock of communities, and always have been. They rarely get announced at a government press conference, and if they did, the opposition would roast them. When have you seen a politician proudly announce that the government helped two families re-open the local grocery store?

WH. Too small potatoes.

JFH: Point number two about our abuse of the ocean and the people who live near it is about Boat Harbour, where the pulp mill spewed effluent into the water for half a century. We have learned to call that environmental racism, when we put the dump next to powerless African or Indigenous communities. Pictou Landing First Nation was there long before the pulp mill, and now its citizens live next to a cesspool, not the fresh salt air they should be enjoying. It took a long time to begin to right those harms to the water and the people. The damage may never completely go away, not to the water nor the people who live beside it.

WH: It must be hard for governments to know what projects to approve, though.

JFH: Sure is, if they consult only with the developers who wouldn't be in the project if they didn't stand to reap big dollars for themselves and their shareholders. Yes, that's how business works; but when we vote in an election we are not giving the winning party *carte blanche* to sell the trees and water out from under us to somebody's shareholders. Our government should not sit on the same side of the table as developers, and against the community. We didn't elect them to rule us, but to do the best for us. I'm not making this up. There was a report produced some years ago for the government, about how we need to promote tourism big-time. Tourism is all about small communities. And natural resources staying natural.

WH: Do you think things will change for the better?

JFH: There must be significant change, or there will be Environment Wars. Either we continue to permit unchecked extraction of all resources until the tides flood the mountains and the lights go out, or – and I much prefer this alternative – those who permit and create environmental destruction will be tried in court and punished. If I bombed or burned a village, wouldn't I be prosecuted and imprisoned? Is it different if my mill or coal mine or oil rig or plant or dump causes the illness or death of citizens or the loss of their food source or clean air or water? Should I not be punished, and swiftly? If I slip poison in someone's food, I'm put in jail. What if my magic beans or big fat fish make people ill because I grow them with poison? Should I go free because I employ the very people I'm poisoning?

WH: There is a dark underbelly to just focusing on the good.

JFH: I love Nova Scotia and I am very grateful for the privilege of living here. I want to keep it good for me. At the same time, I want all my fellow citizens to have access to what I have. Their gains will not mean I lose anything, of that I am certain. We are a small province in Canada, but we're larger than some countries. We can afford to be generous within our borders. We can focus on the possible.

WH: Final thoughts?

JFH: At the end of the book I quoted this mantra from Annette Verschuren's book: *Not bad, not good, only better*. It means that we need to learn about the good and the bad, not so we'll feel good or bad, but so we can do better. I hope this book will help us to do better.

WH: Let's go home now.

JFH: I'm with you.

> People give pain, are callous and insensitive, empty and cruel... but place heals the hurt, soothes the outrage, fills the terrible vacuum that these human beings make.
>
> -- Eudora Welty, 1909-2001, American writer

Appendix

In January 2017 I posted a survey on Facebook and invited my followers to participate and to share it with their followers. I had no other influence over who the respondents would be. One hundred people completed the survey anonymously, from across Canada and beyond. Over the following months, I interviewed twenty-eight current, former, or would-be Nova Scotians, using that survey to guide our conversations.

Here are the survey questions:

1. Where are you 'from,' i.e. where were you born, or where did you grow up, or how do you identify yourself? [community in NS, other Canadian province, USA State, other country]:
2. Where's home for you now? Answer this any way you like.
3. If you live in Nova Scotia, would you ever move away from NS? Why or why not?
4. If you live outside Nova Scotia, would you ever move to / return to Nova Scotia? Why or why not?
5. Are there newcomers in your neighbourhood or community? If so, do you / your neighbours get along with them? Describe how you do or don't.
6. Are you now, or were you ever, a newcomer in a Nova Scotian community? If so, how do / did you get along with your neighbours?
7. Do you have more thoughts on the topics of home and/or Nova Scotia? Did I overlook a question you'd like to answer?

My selection of people to interview was both subjective and random, though I did try to include people from different regions of the province, and minorities. I mostly excluded people who are in the public eye and whose thoughts on any topic may be found elsewhere. I wanted to know what ordinary people thought; I failed at this, as each person I spoke with turned out to be extraordinary.

I took notes manually during our conversations rather than record them, for self-preservation: transcribing recordings is an arduous process. Sometimes I asked people to wait while I finished writing down something pithy they had said. The method is not fool-proof, but I hope I captured the essence of their comments and present them in the spirit in which they were given.

I didn't aim to write a statistical, scientific, touristy, or polemical book. I followed the thoughts and feelings of a virtual community over a period of time. We covered many but by no means all issues that Nova Scotians think about. I aimed to make this interesting and fair, which are challenges enough. Criticize or quote the book as you wish, with this in mind.

Canadian writer Gabrielle Roy is quoted on our 2004 twenty-dollar bills: *Could we ever know each other in the slightest without the arts?* To add dimension to the discussion and help us know each other, I incorporated the works of artists, writers, and a reigning monarch.

Outtakes

These anecdotes didn't find a place in the chapters, but they were too good to leave out:

> *Survey response*
>
> *We moved back when I was ten. We got stopped on the road in the middle of the day by the RCMP because of a gun fight between neighbours...a little unnerving for me as a kid...*

Jessie Hatt met Steven when she was fifteen. She lived in Gold River; he lived just across the river in Chester Basin. They could see each other's homes, but the river was the telephone company's dividing-line between local and long-distance calls, and back in the day long distance was expensive, especially for a fifteen-year-old girl. "So we'd flick the porch lights to say goodnight."

That was common Morse code in the country, before there was texting. A steady porch light meant 'we're home' if other lights were on in the home, or 'we're out' if the house was dark. Flashing porch lights meant 'come home now,' or 'get out of that car and come inside right now,' or 'I'm safely home,' or 'I love you; goodnight.'

If you were told 'I'll leave the porch light on for you,' you knew someone would welcome you, no matter how late you came home, or how long it took you to finally return.

<>

If you grow up in a rural community with generations of your family nearby, your church congregation will be family, too. Kathy Rafuse credits her church family/community with teaching her to play the piano. "I had taken some lessons, so I could read music a bit, but I couldn't play well. They asked me to play for some hymns in church. I got every note wrong, but once the congregation began to sing, they covered what I was doing anyway. After every service, my uncle would say, 'Good playing, Kathy.' So how could I fail? In this way, they taught me to play."

<>

Sandee MacLean says, "I was walking along the road with my husband. A car slows down, an elderly man inquires about our surname. We say MacLean, my husband's family name. The man wants to know more, but when my husband says he's a MacLean from PEI, the man rolls up the window and drives off!"

<>

Fishing boats have a steadying sail on the stern to help keep the bow pointing into the wind when at anchor. Jessie Hatt's sail-maker used blue canvas for hers, but didn't have quite enough material, so added a white strip in the centre. It looked like a feather. Jessie said she is known to some as "Jessie Fishes With a Feather." She loves that name.

<>

Kris Srivatsa quotes a Sanskrit saying about how leadership affects social attitudes: "As is the king, so are the people."

> *Survey response*
>
> *Born and bred Bluenoser. I say this because I am very proud of being a Nova Scotian and I love this province. I promote it every chance I get and defend it if necessary. It is my home.*

Acknowledgements

While I do write in solitude, I certainly didn't write this book alone.

- To the twenty-eight extraordinary people who told me what home means to you, I am indebted for your insights and your trust.
- To the one hundred survey respondents who shared your intimate thoughts anonymously, thank you.
- To the contributors of art and blogs and essays and songs brightening these pages, thank you.
- To Lorri Neilsen Glenn, my wise and gentle writing guide, my deep gratitude and admiration.
- To my sister Margaret MacDonald Trites, aka the grammar queen, thank you for your formidable proofreading skills, and for your constant support.
- To my sister Christine Heggelin, thank you for your beautiful painting on the cover of this book, and for your constant support.
- To all who tossed me a cheerful "It'll be great, you'll see," my thanks. You never know how important such support can be to one who is in the midst of blindly trying to pin the book tail on the publishing donkey.
- The previous comment is not meant to cast aspersions on Moose House Publications, whose impeccable judgment has made it possible for this book to become a real thing.
- To Andrew Wetmore, my editor at Moose House, deep gratitude for making my good book better.

In spite of all efforts, there may be errors. I am very clever at hiding them in plain sight, and take full credit for any that may appear.

Jan Fancy Hull

Index

Jan Fancy Hull

About the author

Jan Fancy Hull lives in a log chalet beside a quiet lake in Lunenburg County, Nova Scotia, where she has written poetry, fiction, and her debut non-fiction book, *Where's Home?* Prior to arriving at this idyllic position, she served in various careers, enterprises, pursuits, and avocations, including, but not limited to, arts administrator, radio broadcaster, sailing tours skipper, and employee benefits broker.

In the warm months, Jan creates sculptures from Nova Scotian sandstone, which she exhibits in various galleries and shows. She is currently active in the Lunenburg Art Society. She also enjoys golfing and drifting around the lake in a tiny rowboat, but doesn't do enough of either. There are so many things to do.

Website: janfancyhull.ca
Facebook: Jan Fancy Hull

Jan Fancy Hull